THE EMPOWERED EMPATH

Become Your Own Shaman

Rev. Dr. Bonnie M. Russell

The Empowered Empath

Become Your Own Shaman

Bonnie M. Russell, DS, DD, MSL, MH

A Blossom Spring Publication

Castro Valley, California, USA

ISBN-13: 978-1717311696

Editing, interior layout and formatting by

Blossom Spring Publications

www.blossomspring.com

Cover Art by B. M. Russell

Dedication

I would like to dedicate this book to Damon Russell for his unfailing support of my quest to heal the world.

The Empowered Empath

Rev. Dr. Bonnie M. Russell

CONTENTS

ACKNOWLEDGMENTS

I would like to thank Rompolo 'Polo' Romero for sharing his knowledge of rain forest plants and his herbal wisdom with me. It was a great adventure knowing you, and I'll miss you always.

"Great Mystery,

Teach me how to trust my head, my mind, my intuition, my inner knowing, the senses of my body, the blessings of my spirit. Teach me to trust these things so that I may enter my Sacred Space and love beyond my fear, and thus walk in balance with the passing of each glorious sun."

~Native American Prayer

The Empowered Empath

A comprehensive guide for making your sensitivities work for you

Introduction

You know you're an empath because you feel things that overwhelm and scare you. You know things about strangers on the street that you have no scientific way to prove. Sometimes these feelings make you anxious or maybe they scare you so much that you have trouble leaving the house. Your home is your refuge… and your prison.

This course is designed to take you from the helplessness and anxiety that accompanies empathy, to the fearlessness of a modern day shaman.

This course is the culmination of all that I have learned from the many healing techniques I have studied, combined with all of the information I have personally gleaned from Spirit while treating clients in my healing practice.

We will learn how disease manifests physically, but is rooted in energy. We will learn to read energy, and restore the flow of energy, to this root.

We will learn that it makes no difference whether or not the client believes in energy therapy because the healer is not communicating with their conscious mind. The healer communicates with the subconscious mind, or Blessed Higher Self, to clear karma and energetic blocks to wholeness.

We will understand that learning to be your own shaman does not interfere with any religion. In fact, the skills we will learn in this class will enhance and deepen your connection to God, the Divine, and the Universal Source of all.

One possible exception is this: *You will come to know that we are all one, and in order to heal, we must love everyone and everything.*

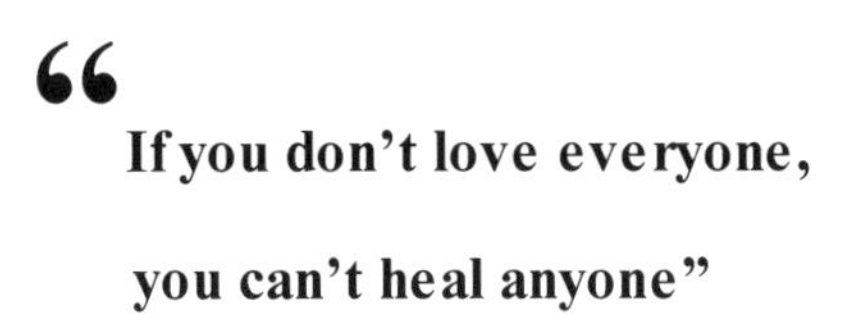

“ If you don’t love everyone,

you can’t heal anyone”

Our 6th sense is something we were all born with, just like the other five; sight, hearing, touch, taste and smell. In this course, we will focus on increasing our perception of the world around us with our intuition. The goal is that we learn to experience the world around us with all six senses, equally.

If you find that you are uncomfortable with such terms as “meditation”, “medium”, “past life regression”, “séance”, and even the use of the word “energy”, I implore you to think of these terms, as just words. They are totally powerless until we assign meaning to them. In this course, these terms are all used with the strict purpose of bringing healing to ourselves and our clients.

We will learn to converse with spirits on the Other Side because there are higher beings with valuable information for healing who are eager for us to be able to hear them. They have absolutely no interest in our beliefs. They are there whether we believe in them or not.

In the end, we will know that all healing comes from Love, which is the highest energetic frequency on the planet, and we will know how to match our personal vibration, and that of our clients, to this frequency. This is known as harmony and it is the destination of all who are on the path to enlightenment.

As you embark upon this journey to discover the greatest secrets of the Universe I would like to give you the biggest key to the whole process, right here, right at the beginning:

Don't take yourself too seriously.

That's it. Relax and let yourself enjoy the process. All of the greatest enlightened beings from around the globe laugh easily and enjoy life to the fullest. If these incredible, intelligent, grounded people see this world as a wondrous playground, shouldn't we?

The answers are within

I am a natural born intuitive, and so are you. The reason we don't know this is because we were either taught to forget, or have had our 'imaginations' trained out of us by our parents, society or church. Think back to some of your earliest memories and you'll likely remember playing with imaginary friends, being completely comfortable in situations that made your parents uneasy or even quiet moments spent watching the subtle movements of energy in nature. Things like the way dry leaves move across the pavement in a gust of wind or the way branches sway in the trees up above. These simple facinations lead us to discover so much about ourselves and the ways of energy, yet when we get caught observing these simple things, we're told to stop daydreaming.

It is my intention to help you remember how to to sense energies and see auras and spirits.

When we come into this world we are still so connected to the Other Side, that we can converse easily with those who are still there. Think about how many children have imaginary friends, then ask yourself how this could possibly be a coincidence.

The reason some of us retain knowledge of the Other Side as we grow older is because we dedicated ourselves to higher consciousness in previous lifetimes and that is also the reason you are holding this book in your hands right now. You retained some bit of your prior knowledge of your Universal consciousness and now are seeking to remember more.

You will find answers to the questions your soul is searching for. You will come to see that your sensitivities to the emotions of others is a gift, not a detriment, and certainly nothing to be afraid of. Rather, it is a super power and you need to learn how to make it work for you.

Here are some simple definitions of terms I'll be using throughout the course. We will get deeper into these things as we move along.

Blessed Higher Self or **BHS**: This is your sub-concious mind, your higher mind or that part of you that is in constant communication with the Other Side, our guides and Universal Source.

Collective Unconscious: Synonomous with God. Used when we refer to thoughts and inspiration from a supernatural origin.

Empath: a person with the paranormal ability to apprehend the mental or emotional state of another individual.

Great Spirit: Synonomous with God.

Other Side: Simply put, this is home. The place we all originated from and will return to. The religious minded call it Heaven.

Medical Intuitive: A medical intuitive is an alternative medicine practitioner who uses their intuitive abilities to find the cause of a physical or emotional condition. Other terms for such a person include medical clairvoyant, medical psychic or intuitive counselor.

Red Road: Native American phrase for Spiritual path.

Sensitive: A person who is believed to respond to supernatural influences. Quick to detect or respond to slight changes, signals, or influences. (You can be sensitive without being emotional)

Universal Source (Source Energy): Synonomous with God.

White Light: The highest, purest energy; Love. It is used to surround and protect ourselves and it comes from the balance of our chakras (which represent every color in the rainbow), creating a clean, clear connection to our Universal Source.

Something I will also be refering to often is the Love - Fear scale. If we think of these two in terms of a vibrational frequency, fear will be at the very bottom of the scale, while the frequency of pure love vibrates right off the top. It has no limits and when we are connected to and working from the highest level of love, that is where, when and how miracles happen.

When we are in the flow of the higher vibrations, everthing works out. We call this being in *alignment*. When we are going through hard times and vibrating on the lower registers of the scale, we are out of alignment and instead, are in a state of *resistance*.

We can also think of it like this: Cold is not a measurable energy, rather it is the absence of heat. Heat is the energy form that is lacking from the room or object, making it cold. Think of the thermostat on your wall. When you adjust the temperature, you are adjusting the amount of heat that your furnace will create. When we feel cold, we turn up the heat.

When we talk about vibrational frequency, all there is is Love. When there is a shortage of love, we experience fear, but fear is not an energy form all by itself. It is simply a lack of love.

When we have ill will towards others and experience sickness in our bodies, those fear based states are signals telling us we need to 'turn up the love'.

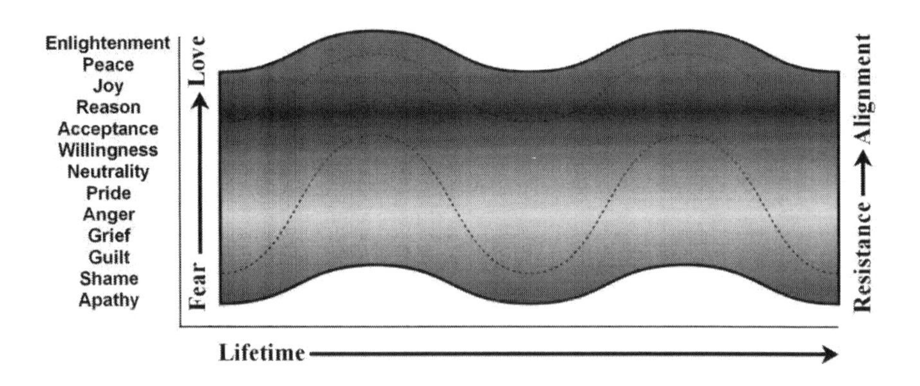

The dotted line that bounces between the red and the lower parts of the blue, represents someone who lives with anxiety, depression and chronic illness. The dotted line in the upper portion of the diagram represents a person who is in the flow of love and is aligned closely with Source Energy.

An empath can read your energy when he or she lives in the flow and is in alignment. A true psychic is really just someone who knows how to tap into the collective unconscious at will.

Now ask yourself these questions:

Have you ever seen a ghost? Heard your name called from 'nowhere'? Smelled roses in the dead of winter? Or had some other super-natural experience?

It was during these moments that you were without resistance. You where in clear alignment with the Universal Source.

The Empowered Empath

Become your own Shaman

What is a Shaman?

Shaman: noun The word 'Shaman,' is actually a Tungus (Siberian) word for a spiritual practice that is as old as mankind, and is still practiced by indigenous people, as well as modern practitioners worldwide. Shamanism is not rooted in any organized religious tradition, but is instead a system of controlled visionary journeys into alternate realities (and back,) in order to contact spirit guides and gain their assistance in divination and healing.

A Shaman is someone who is trained in:

- **MIND:** Counseling, hypnosis, meditation and relaxation techniques.

- **BODY:** Natural medicine such as herbs, vitamins, and nutrition.

- **SPIRIT:** Ministry encompassing Marriages, Baptisms, and all rites of passage.

Everything under one, holistic, umbrella

Ultimately you will come to understand that a Shaman is someone who uses all of this knowledge with one foot in this world and one on the Other Side.

The purpose of becoming your own shaman, is to claim your power and to acknowledge your responsibility for your own life. It is also to obtain enlightenment, which will bring us closer to the perfecting of our spirits. That is the purpose and meaning of life. It is also to be an example to the world that it is possible to be happy and healthy and fulfilled in this lifetime.

What's Your Story?

I'm going to paraphrase Caroline Myss, as she used this analogy once and it really resonated with me:

Let's look at the levels of consciousness as the floors, or stories, of a big city apartment building.

We all start out on the first floor and many of us never live in the Penthouse.

We have the same address as the people in the penthouse, but we have a different view. To those living on the ground level, the ocean is miles away; to the penthouse dwellers, it's right outside their window. On the first floor we have pollution; garbage on the street, and a constant stream of noise, traffic and sirens. In the Penthouse, it's peaceful and quiet. Down by the street we lock our windows against thieves, while there is no need for that on the upper floors.

It is our choice which floor we live on, but with each choice, the mortgage gets higher. Our costs increase. Most of us want to live on the upper floors, but we ground ourselves with negative thoughts about what it takes to get there.

As we move up to higher stories, we get new neighbors. We lose some of our old friends who are stuck in their first floor mentality, but we gain new friends who have similar goals.

When we see the next staircase, we know the risks, and we start pacing because we understand there's going to be a price. But we start thinking about the reward and we must decide. We KNOW we 're going to take that flight up, it's just a matter of when.

Once that inner spiritual appetite wakes up, we can't help but go up.

As we progress story by story, the more our appetites change from a desire for exterior things, to interior things.

On the first floor we want stuff and money and physical beauty, but as we make our way up to the penthouse, we want to give, rather than take. We ask, "What can I become? What do I have within me that is spectacular?" We become the subject of our investigation instead of worrying about what everyone else is doing.

When we live in the lower levels, the way we perceive problems, crisis, relationships, illness, is to go to an outside person and say, "You, fix me". I am a victim. I didn't deserve this. It *happened* to me. And our other first floor friends gather around and say, "It's not fair! She needs our help to…" raise money, hold her hand, blame God, whatever. And on the first level, God is a God of democracy. He only allows bad things to happen to bad people. If we haven't broken any laws, we should not be punished, and we may think of some bad people who should be sick instead.

As we climb up the Spiritual staircase, we begin to take responsibility for ourselves. We watch what we say, and then we learn to watch what we think. Our reality begins to change for the better, because we are putting better things out into the world. This is how energy (karma) works; we reap what we sow. Probably the best thing about doing this very hard work on ourselves, is that every spiritual step we take is cumulative. Every hurdle we cross stays crossed. When we reach those upper floors, the knowledge stays with us for not only this lifetime, but through all others. Forever.

How to read this book

This is a texbook and is designed to be used as an eight week course. You will find that each chapter begins with the words, “Week One”, Week Two”, and so on. To get the most from this book you must commit to reading it in this fashion, doing all the exercises and homework, and not reading ahead.

I recommend that you choose a time to read that you can stick to each week. Are Sunday mornings good for you? Great! Read the first lesson in its entirety and do the homework, then next Sunday morning read the second lesson, and so on.

I’ve been teaching this course in the classroom for several years and I’ve found that metering out the information in this way is the most effective method to reach our goals.

It also teaches the importance of self-discipline. If you can follow directions AND use your intuition, you can rule the world!

I will talk to the reader as if you yourself are a teacher or healer. The reason I do this is because we are all teachers and healers. The information in this book is to be shared so it can grow enough to heal us all so I want you to imagine yourself sharing these skills as you are learning them.

There is absolutely no room for competition on the path to enlightenment. We are in this together. I will share the inspiring words of other masters with you, and you will share the pearls you glean from books, lectures and your own intuition with those you know and love.

I encourage you to start classes in your living room or public library, using this book as a guide to create a healthy community.

This course will change your perception of reality!

Week One
Claim your Power, Claim your Joy!

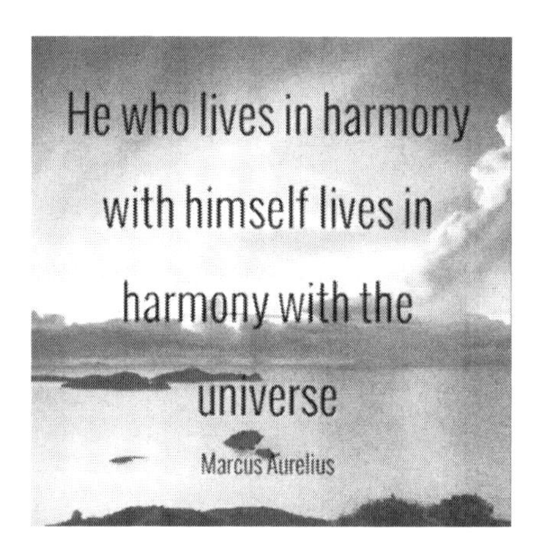

You matter.

I've been on all the internet pages and groups for empaths and they all tend to have really bad habits among the members; we whine and complain. A typical post that I often see is, "Does anyone else feel this heavy energy lately? I can't sleep and I feel so depressed". These posts are then followed by hundreds of "me too" comments and no actual strategies to deal with it. Some people will suggest grounding or meditation, but nobody wants to be the voice of reason and say, "Quit it! You are more powerful than this!"

I consider this book to be my voice, finally saying "Quit it!!"

The Universal Source of all things, God, the Great Spirit, does not make mistakes. We were made to feel things so we can change them. A shamanic truth is that we will never be shown something we cannot change. In this course you will learn how to change what you see from something unproductive into something useful.

We all have baggage. We have had painful experiences and

some of us come from backgrounds of abuse or neglect, but we all have to learn how to cope with our pasts so that we may move forward. As you embark on the journey of empowerment, it is important to know who *you* are, so that you can make the distinction between your energy, thoughts and emotions, and those of others.

Choosing to take back your power happened the day you stepped onto the spiritual path, or as the Native Americans call it, the Red Road.

How do I claim my power?

- *Make a conscious shift in your thinking*, from caring for others first, to caring for yourself first. Here's the difference: When you put others first, you never get your turn, but when you put yourself first, not only are you caring for your own needs, but you will find that you have an increased capacity to give.
- *Morning meditation is a way to charge your spirit for the day*. Get in touch with your inner wants and needs before ever leaving your bed. Typically when we wake up our minds begin to bombard us with our to-do list and if we jump up and start doing stuff, we begin the day off balance. Take five or ten minutes (a snooze cycle on your alarm is perfect!) to ground all those thoughts and consciously connect to your Source. We'll learn more about that next week, but for this week I want you to trust your instincts and connect using your instincts. Don't look ahead!
- *Daily Yoga, Pilates, or some type of gentle stretching and exercise* is key for producing that "feel good" release of endorphins. When you do this every day it empowers you, clears your mind, and actually gives you energy.

• *Make healthy dietary choices.* Organic, whole foods will be completely utilized by your body, and they will make you feel good. Become an instinctive eater, rather than following a strict diet. Remember, your BHS knows what is best for you.

• *Become an active observer.* Spend time exploring the things you like and dislike. Many times we choose things for ourselves without giving it much thought. Think about your wardrobe. Do you like the clothes you have on, or did you just grab what fits? What's your favorite color? Do you love your homes furnishings? Making these observations will give you a greater sense of self.

• *What are your sexual preferences*? This is a difficult subject for some, but one that is becoming easier to explore with the changing times. The LGBTQ movement has made powerful changes in the general public's perceptions about sexuality, making it easier to discuss with our partners and with the whole world, if we feel so inclined. Explore your likes and dislikes and ask yourself if you are who you are because it was your choice, or because of societal pressures to conform.

• *Give yourself permission to set your own personal pace*. You may feel that a friend is progressing faster than you are, but you have a physical and emotional need to avoid stress and pressure. Do what works for you. This is a life lesson that cannot be stressed enough! As you progress on the Red Road you will find yourself coming back to the same issues over and over if you don't take the time to patiently listen to the lesson at hand the first time around.

• *Even well-meaning people will say insensitive things*. Don't read too much into hurtful comments. Chances are you'll give more energy to their ill measured words, than they intended to convey, and besides, it is none of your business what other people think of you. Only you know what is in your heart. Choose to spend time with people who allow you to be yourself when you're with them, and don't cause you to worry about their motives.

• *Communicate clearly.* When you explain yourself thoroughly and completely, you leave it entirely up to your audience to either a) understand you, or b) misconstrue the facts. But, because you communicated your thoughts clearly, you can be sure the Universe will see things through. Some of us may think we're good communicators but if we are not answering these six questions when we convey information, we're not being 'complete'. The questions are who? What? Where? When? Why? And how? Examine the next email or text you type to be sure you're giving all the critical information to your reader.

• *You cannot change the people around you.* You only have control over your own reactions to them. If you have communicated properly and still face opposition, remember these phrases: "I bless you in your truth" or "Nameste" are very empowering statements. They allow you to send love to heal the situation, while allowing you to move on.

• *Vocalize your appreciation.* Tell people when you appreciate them. Say, "I love you" to someone every day. If someone does a good job, tell them. When we share our hearts with the people we care about, it increases our own vibration and creates feelings of self-worth.

• *Listen more than you speak.* It's not all about you. In social settings, and in your healing practice, ask questions and listen carefully to the answers. Listening will help you to realize who you are, what your likes and dislikes are, far more than retelling your own story ever will. Bonus: People love to talk about themselves. If you're a good listener, your company will be sought after!

• *Guilt is a choice.* It is something we allow, or refuse to allow. We can choose to take it upon ourselves, or see it for what it is; a tool used by others to control us. No one can *make* you feel guilty, so don't accept guilt in your life. Guilt can be debilitating if we let it. It can be the cause of stunted growth in many areas of life. The ill measured words of controlling parents, grandparents, spiritual leaders and teachers can be the cause of every issue that we, as adults, now struggle to overcome. We must learn to see these words as outside of ourselves and refuse ownership of them. For instance, if your mother says that you never call her, gently remind her that the phone works both ways.

• *You are more than just what you see in the mirror*. When you have setbacks, and begin to feel down about yourself, remember that you are so much more than just this physical body. Learn to detach your higher self from your physical self with meditation. (We'll learn more about that next week. This week just do your best)

• *Affirmations are a powerful tool*. Use them. "I am a complete and perfect creation" is a great place to start. Post this, or something like it, in places you're likely to see it often, such as your cars dashboard, your kitchen cabinet, and on your desk at work. Write your own, more specific affirmations, as your personal goals change. If you've ever used any of my Blossom Spring® herbal remedies, you've probably noticed that each one comes with an affirmation. That's how firmly I believe in their healing power.

• *Nightly Review is a great habit to get into*. Start a daily journal in which you will write about the things you achieved that day. This is where you pat yourself on the back for channeling stress effectively, holding your tongue when you really wanted to scream, and all the little things you did for yourself that changed the way you see yourself.

- *Your personal Power is anchored in your integrity.* Tell the truth, keep your word, and never engage in gossip. Don't speak it, and don't listen to it. Maintaining your integrity will keep you centered and healthy.

Claiming your Power is about knowing who you are, and the choices you make every day. It is my sincerest goal, that through this course, you will resonate with that truth, and reconnect with the ancient knowledge that is already within your Blessed Higher Self.

Exercise: Write what each color means to you next to it in the list below. How does it make you feel? What does it smell like? Taste like? Note anything at all that occurs to you. The meaning of this exercise will be explained at the end of this chapter.

Black

White

Red

Orange

Yellow

Green

Turquoise

Blue

Purple

Feeling and Seeing Energy

Let's practice feeling energy. Start by holding your hands together in the prayer position, fingers straight and there should be tension from your fingertips to your wrists, and maybe all the way to your elbows. Now move them an inch away from one another, maintaining that tension. Focus on the space between your hands and you will begin to feel a sensation very much like the sensation you get when trying to push two magnets together the wrong way. Now move your hands back and forth a little bit to increase that sensation. Pretty neat, right?

Our hands are most sensitive to the subtle energies and that's why we use our hands to help us sense the energy fields of others. Move your hands further apart and you'll notice the sensation begins to diminish until… you move them back and forth like you did before. The sensation is actually stronger, isn't it?

If you are doing this course with someone else, take turns passing a hand or an object through the beam of energy your partner has between their hands. Again, the active hands will have some tension to them. For example, if you raise your hand to wave to someone, your hand is mostly limp, but if you are readying yourself to catch a ball, the tension I'm talking about will be present in your hand.

Take note of the properties of the beam your partner has created. How does it feel to you? How does it feel to them? Discuss the weight and temperature and anything else you notice about the differences between the beam of energy and the space outside of the beam.

If you are doing this course with a group, position two people at opposite ends of the room and have them each raise a palm and face them toward each other.

When they can both tell you that they feel the energy between the upraised palms, have the other students take turns passing their hands through the beam and discuss the different sensations felt and observed by all.

Grounding

Now that you have felt the amazing energy that flows through and around the body, let's take a moment to ground ourselves. What this means is, we're going to reign in and get some semblance of control over all that energy we just played with. When we ground the energy, what we are actually doing is centering and balancing ourselves so we can move on with the day.

An easy way to do this is to get quiet and take three slow, deep breaths. With each breath, imagine yourself becoming calm and centered as any frenetic, or extra, energy that you have hanging around drains out of your body and into the earth through the soles of your feet.

Once you feel complete, like everything has been released, place the thumb of your right hand into the palm of your left hand and close your fingers around your thumb. Next, press them into the body, at the sternum.

This is what we call a *trigger*. A trigger is used when we want to recall a sense memory quickly. Because you created this trigger, you can recall this feeling of calm in an instant any time you are experiencing stress.

White Light

After working with energy, then grounding and centering yourself, you'll want to 'seal it in' by surrounding yourself with White Light. We will talk about this more in the coming weeks, but for now, think of it as a force field full of protective Universal Energy. Close your eyes and imagine your body completely surrounded by this white light so that to an outside observer, you seem to be inside of a big white egg. When you see and feel it all around you, surround the white light with a shell like a force field. When you feel like it is nice and solid you are complete and you may open your eyes.

A word about The 2012 Energies

After much study, contemplation, and meditation, this is what I've come to understand about the new era, and how to get through the transition:

We need to:

1- Ask ourselves who we are and why we're here. Examine our thoughts on life and death, and seek to connect with our Blessed Higher Self.

2- Align your personal will with Divine Will. Accept and trust in what life brings you moment to moment.

3- List your fears and act in spite of them. Don't worry about being perceived as different or eccentric.

4- Understand, and then break through your traditional and/or religious conditioning. Look for the answers within yourself. Do not try to find them in any book or from any teacher.

5- Strive to learn lessons from every life situation.

6- Be honest with yourself and others, and take responsibility for your thoughts and actions. This clears karma!

7- Live each day as if it was your last day on earth, because all that matters; all that is really real, is the present moment.

We are going through difficult times; people are losing their jobs, their homes, and longtime relationships. Through these trials, our true nature is being revealed, not only to ourselves, but to those around us. And it's happening very quickly. Where it once took years to figure out that your business partner was a liar and a cheat, these things are now coming to the surface with surprising clarity and speed. The opposite is true as well, those whose lives are heart centered, and well intentioned are just as easy to spot. We are all becoming transparent, and this is a huge blessing!

Think about the current state of our world. How did we become so greedy? When did things become more important than people? This energy shift needs to happen in order for us to remember who we are and what it is we're supposed to be doing with our lives. We are being shaken, and the cream is rising to the top, ready or not. With every passing day, in every situation, grasp the opportunity to learn something new about yourself, and the people around you. Recognize the people who are not aligned with your spirit path, and watch as they either self-destruct, or simply fall away from your life. You won't need to lift a finger.

Some have taught that December 21, 2012 is the end of the world, but we know this: We're still here! Science has proven that infinity applies to all things; every molecule. The so called end of the world is not a mathematical possibility. It's not a literal end of the world, but rather the end of an age. We have left the Age of Pisces behind, (which began with the birth of Christ and ended when 2012 came to a close), into the Age of Aquarius, which we began to feel emerging around 1965. (There was a 40 some year overlap, and we are alive during this shift!)

The transition, from one Age to the next, simply means that it is "the end of life" as we know it, and isn't that a good thing?

Matter can change form, and catastrophes have always occurred throughout time, but life (energy) goes on forever. Even the Holy Bible's account of the end of times is called the book of Revelation, which means something new being revealed. New information unveiled for a new way of life.

I encourage everyone to have faith in yourselves and believe in your own strength. You can do this by becoming a treasure hunter within your own Spirit. Mine for the golden nuggets within, and after you've examined the 'dirt' that we all inevitably find, glean whatever lesson from it that you can, bless it, and toss it aside. Forgive yourself for mistakes, and reach for tomorrows many opportunities to grow. Learn about, and come to love, the perfect creation that you are becoming.

Exercise: I had you write what the colors feel and mean to you so that later, when they come up in readings, you will have already defined your interpretations. Other teachers like to tell you what the colors mean, but only you can discern what Spirit is telling you. For example, if you see the color red in a reading about the amazing love you feel between two people, the red in this instance signifies that love, even if red means fear or hate to someone else. So, if you have memorized the meanings of colors from any source outside of yourself, forget them.

Homework

1. **Daily Meditation** – Any time of day, for 10-20 minutes a day.

2. **Nightly Review** – Each night, write down 5 positive things that happened during the day. Either things that you saw, things that happened to you, goals you accomplished or good deeds that you did.

Suggested Reading: At the end of each week you will find resources for deepening your understanding of the subject matter we just covered.

Practical Intuition -Laura Day

Why People Don't Heal and How They Can -Carolyn Myss, MI

Celestine Prophesies – James Redfield

Meditation

Week Two

Why We Meditate

A psychologist walked around a room while teaching stress management to an audience. As she raised a glass of water, everyone expected they'd be asked the "half empty or half full" question. Instead, with a smile on her face, she inquired: "How heavy is this glass of water?" Answers called out ranged from 8 oz. to 20 oz. She replied, "The absolute weight doesn't matter. It depends on how long I hold it. If I hold it for a minute, it's not a problem. If I hold it for an hour, I'll have an ache in my arm. If I hold it for a day, my arm will feel numb and paralyzed. In each case, the weight of the glass doesn't change, but the longer I hold it, the heavier it becomes." She continued, "The stresses and worries in life are like that glass of water. Think about them for a while and nothing happens. Think about them a bit longer and they begin to hurt. And if you think about them all day long, you will feel paralyzed – incapable of doing anything."

When we meditate, we are putting the glass down.

5 Myths about Meditation

1. Meditation is too difficult.

Many people assume that meditation is too hard or difficult. This is simply not true. Meditation is a simple as sitting down and breathing, nothing else.

2. Meditation takes too long, I'm too busy, I don't have the time to meditate.

A simple meditation practice can take between 5-30 minutes. Depending on the time you have available on any given day, fitting meditation into your lifestyle is an easy change.

3. Meditation is a religious activity.

Practicing meditation does not conflict with any religious beliefs. Of course there are many people who use a meditation practice for religious reasons. A meditation practice is simply the cessation of the chatter in the mind, and can be used by all people of any religion.

4. Meditation is hard to learn.

Following simple instructions or a guided meditation can enable you to slowly begin to train the mind and body for meditation. With little practice you will be ready to begin to meditate on your own.

5. Meditation is way too boring. I'm too inattentive and I can't sit still that long, so I can't meditate.

As with any new endeavor at first you might find it hard to sit still or keep the mind focused by you will quickly learn to calm the mind and body. Cultivating a mindfulness practice through meditation while using your breath will allow you to learn to sit and be still.

We meditate to achieve Spiritual Enlightenment

Meditation will not eliminate the causes of stress or discomfort, but it will change the way we think about stressful and uncomfortable things. We meditate to transcend suffering by shifting our perspective from the mundane, to our Oneness with all things. This shifts the importance we place on discomfort by enabling us to create a healthy disconnect from everyday stuff. It allows us to disengage from the cognitive & emotional and activate the higher mind. To do this we must familiarize ourselves with the energy of everyday things so we will be able to discern between the energy we emit, versus the energies we are surrounded by.

Thoughts have energy, and that energy affects the physical body. When we have appreciative thoughts about ourselves, we create health, and conversely, when we focus on the things we dislike about ourselves, we are essentially inviting those things to continue to decline.

The following experiment was conducted by Dr. Masaru Emoto. In his book, "Messages from Water" he shows the effect that thoughts have on water. Keep in mind that the human body is more than 80% water.

Energetically infused water molecules

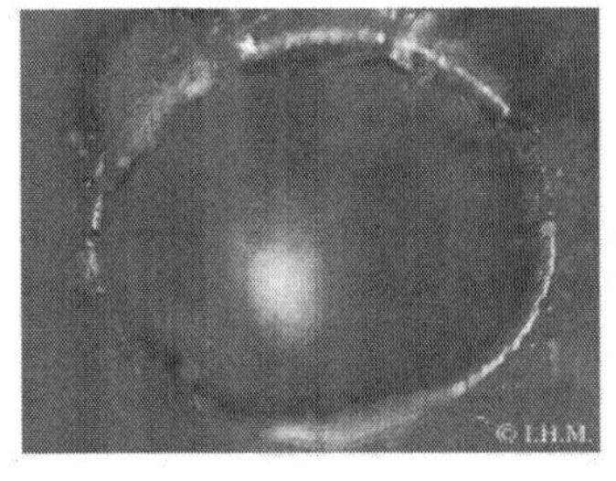

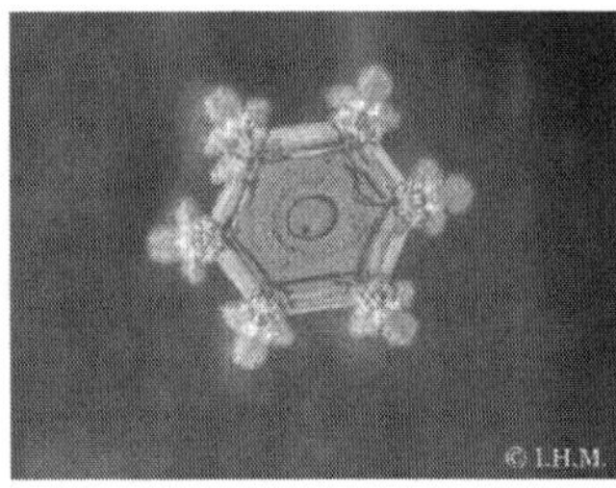

The energy of *"Fear & distrust"* and the energy of *"Love & gratitude"*

Sound has the ability to change our moods quickly and profoundly. Low energy music keeps us in very low levels of physical and mental health. Some examples are hateful lyrics, disharmonious notes that sound chaotic and out of sync, and notes on the low vibratory scale, such as drums. However, when we immerse ourselves in higher energy music, with beautiful harmonies which incorporate a spectrum of sounds in balance, from drums, to pianos, to flutes, we feel the uplifting quality throughout our being. To enhance this energy further, such as for the purpose of meditation, we listen to only high energy instrumentals, such as harps, flutes and bells. I always play "Ardas", from the Crimson Series, during healing sessions and for meditation. Ardas is prayer beyond prayer and it acts as a catalyst to the higher dimensions.

Light and color also have a profound effect on our energy. Seasonal Affective Disorder, or SAD, is a very real malady that is a type of depression. It affects people living at latitudes near the north and south poles, because they have very little sunlight during the winter. Their doctors prescribe light therapy to brighten their moods. Likewise, it is vitally important to have open curtains and/or windows in our living spaces, and to paint with light or bright colors. Then consider your wardrobe. Wearing light and bright colors has an uplifting effect, while wearing dark colors, especially tops, shirts, and jackets, which are near our face, can contribute to bad or sad moods.

All of these things have a subconscious effect on us at the cellular level. Be aware of the thoughts, colors and sounds you surround yourself with.

The Gap

Meditation consciously bridges the gap between the physical particles of the body; the cells that can be seen under a microscope, and the spiritual, energetic body, which is the intelligence that binds those particles together. It creates the connection between the mind and the body. It is in this space that we actually, literally, create the physical body that we inhabit.

Every cell in the body is covered with little pockets that are called receptors, and these receptors collect chemicals from the brain, (along with oxygen from the lungs, and vitamins and minerals from the food we eat) via the bloodstream for our nourishment. When we are depressed, we create very low levels of serotonin, our happy juice, and dopamine, our satisfaction detector. The cells in our body change in response to this deficiency by making fewer receptors, leading to malnutrition, decay and atrophy.

Serotonin is thought to be especially active in constricting smooth muscles, transmitting impulses between nerve cells, regulating cyclic body processes and contributing to wellbeing and happiness. Serotonin is regarded by some researchers as the chemical that is responsible for maintaining mood balance, and that a deficit of serotonin leads to depression.

Dopamine is a neurotransmitter that helps control the brain's reward and pleasure centers. Dopamine also helps regulate movement and emotional responses, and it enables us not only to see rewards, but to take action to move toward them. Dopamine deficiency results in Parkinson's Disease, and people with low dopamine activity may be more prone to addiction. The absence of a certain kind of dopamine receptor is also associated with sensation-seeking people, more commonly known as "risk takers."

However, when we are happy and surround ourselves with the

energy of pure love, these receptors increase, leading to healthy, well nourished, vibrant cell structures.

Meditation literally, physically, changes our bodies in a very real way.

How to Manifest Abundance

Manifesting is easy. Everyone manifests all the time. The sad fact is most people are really good at manifesting what they don't want.

To manifest abundance you have to keep your mind on the abundance you want and off everything else. This is very hard to do because during the course of the day your mind has over 50,000 thoughts. Most of these thoughts are useless and repetitive. Most of these thoughts you don't want running through your head.

The concept is simple but in practice it becomes hard because our minds want to run wild. We may start out keeping our minds on something we want to manifest like abundance but then during the course of the day our thoughts drift.

But that is only half of the problem.

To really manifest abundance we must use our hearts as well. We must create a feeling of well-being with our hearts. This will create an electromagnetic field which will align itself with the universe which will in turn align itself with our intent.

Now we go back to the 50,000 thoughts which our interrupting our intent. Not only are these 50,000 thoughts keeping our minds off what we want but also our heart from feeling what we need to feel to manifest abundance.

The heart and the mind have to work in union. If they are not working together we will not manifest abundance.

Most people do not manifest abundance because they can't go through the course of the day and keep their mind on what they want to and their heart feeling the necessary emotions. They think they are not manifesting. But they are. You are constantly manifesting those things which hold your attention the most.

Until you find a way to control your mind and center on your heart you will be at the mercy of the 50,000 thoughts you have every day. Thoughts you are unaware of. This truly puts you at the mercy of the unknown.

Learn to control your thoughts and you can manifest abundance today.

Aligning yourself with new 5th dimension energies

Spiritual energy, commonly referred to as 5th Dimension energy, has been increasing in both volume and frequency since the close of 2012. Many people have been experiencing sensations that range from, serious illness to dizziness, and just feeling "spaced out", or an inability to get organized, to relationship troubles and loss of employment and/or homes. It is vital to our well-being to assimilate these frequencies.

There are two types of meditation which I have found useful for this purpose.

Transcendental Meditation (TM), in which the focus is on breath and having a clear mind. Free of all thoughts and distractions, it is valuable for downloading new frequencies and information. In TM a trans-like state is achieved when we reach a place of selflessness. It is only through TM that we fully understand that we are *all one*. In the nothingness of a TM trance we have no ego. We simply float in the high vibration of love, which brings perfection to every cell in our bodies.

Guided meditation is used to consciously align with the new 5th dimension energies that are being downloaded into our sub-consciousness. To do this, we focus our meditation on the specific things in our lives that are out of alignment, with the purpose of bringing balance to them.

Mala beads can be used to imprint affirmations into the subconscious mind by repeating your positive statement (mantra) 108 times, which is the number of beads on a mala. This is a very simple way to relieve stress and program yourself with an intention. Holding your mala across your palm, hold the first bead between your thumb and the side of your middle finger (not the index or 'ego' finger), state your mantra, then pull the bead into your hand and hold onto the next bead. Example: Repeating the phrase, "I am perfectly healthy" 108 times will resonate with, and make a physical change in your body. However, saying, "I refuse to be sick anymore" imprints the concept of 'sick' into your cells which will create a negative end result, so always phrase your mantra with care.

You can then wear the mala to keep your intention near your heart and on your mind. If you find yourself reverting back to thoughts of, "I'm sick", meditate on your mala again. Doing the complete chain several times a day will concrete your desire into your cells. It is interesting to note that although, technically this is a guided meditation method, it can become transcendental as you slip into the hypnotic rhythm of your mantra.

A traditional mantra used for the purpose of enlightenment is "Om-mani-padme-hum". Each of the six syllables represents a specific thought, emotion and even has a different color association. It is considered the perfect, complete meditation.

Om Mani Padme Hum meaning

Syllable	Virtue	Purifies	Color
Om	Generosity	Pride/Ego	White
Ma	Ethics	Jealousy	Green
Ni	Patience	Passion	Yellow
Pad	Diligence	Ignorance	Blue
Me	Renunciation	Greed	Red
Hum	Wisdom	Hatred	Black

Handling Personal Conflict

If you have a problem with another person, meditate on their face and everything about them that you love. Hold only high energy thoughts of blessings for them and healing. Surround the person with White Light of protection, and when you feel nothing but love for them, your meditation is complete. Problems with them will now diminish or disappear completely because you have harmonized your energy with theirs in love & light.

When dealing with negative things, such as illness, meditate on the condition by sending your awareness into the body. Look at the organs or tissues that are affected by the malady, and send them love and light. If you perceive any disharmony in the cells, or see any darkness to indicate illness, visualize your white blood cells multiplying and going to work on removing the darkness. See them simply coming through the area and taking the darkness with them to be excreted as waste. When everything seems clean and healthy again, surround the area with protective White Light to 'seal' the work you've just done.

"

When we know, not believe, that we are one with Universal Love,

our vibrational frequency becomes so high that illness cannot touch us.

It is our belief in illness that makes us sick."

Basic Meditation script

This meditation is used when you simply wish to connect to your Blessed Higher Self and the Universe in an effort to receive whatever messages they may have for you, as opposed to meditating on something specific.

You can begin by sitting in a comfortable chair and closing your eyes. Sit with your back straight, and with your feet flat on the floor. Hands rested in your lap.

Take 3 to 5 deep breaths and let your body relax. Feel your energy settle into the moment.

Allow ideas or phrases to emerge into your consciousness from within. Phrases that are big and general enough to encompass all things, and all life everywhere.

Classical examples are "May I live in safety. May I be happy and feel love. May I be healthy. May I live a life of ease."

Repeat these phases, or your own, over and over again. Allow your mind to rest in them. If your attention wanders, don't worry about it. Simply begin again.

"May I live in Safety, be happy, feel love, be healthy, live with ease."

Think of someone you care about; good friend or someone who has helped you or someone who inspires you. Visualize them, say their name to yourself. Get a feeling for their presence, then direct these phrases to them. Imagine them sitting with you then offer these phrases of kindness:

"May *you* live in safety", etc.

Think of someone who is struggling. Offer them these phrases.

When we connect with these phrases, aiming the hearts energies in this way, we're opening ourselves to the possibility of including and connecting, caring and love. Ultimately, we open ourselves to all beings everywhere, without distinction or separation. All people, all animals, everything in existence, known to us and unknown, leaving no one and nothing out. May all beings live in safety, be happy, feel love, be healthy, and live with ease.

Once you have connected completely with these energies, you are vibrating at a very high frequency and you are prepared to receive messages from higher sources, such as your BHS, Angels, guides and masters.

When you feel complete, you may open your eyes and, gently, return to the room.

Signs of Enlightenment

"My Creator, today let me remember the reason I'm here on Mother Earth. Let me look into my own eyes and see the beauty You have created. Let me have good thoughts. Being Indian is not the color of my skin. Being Indian is to listen to my heart, to think only the things You have taught, to watch nature and live in harmony. Being Indian is to walk in prayer, to talk to You constantly during the day. Being Indian is to act and to walk in a sacred way."

--Mathew King, LAKOTA

These are the subtle, and not so subtle, signals from the Universe that you are awakening to the new energies that are coming in this year.

1- *Sleeplessness.* This occurs because your physical body is processing these energies more in your sleep, than in your conscious waking hours. Your Blessed Higher Self has decided that it's time for this expansion to occur for you, and it is beginning to give your conscious mind subtle hints.

2- *You will begin to sense the new vibrations.* You may feel tingling or pressure on your crown, and you will experience flashes of inspiration. You will get ideas that you know did not come from inside your own mind. These are signs that your crown is opening to receive the energies.

3- *You may experience waves of emotion.* Simply pause to acknowledge them as they come, then let them pass.

4- *Old issues will come back* to haunt you, and you may feel very lost. You are never lost! These things are coming up so you can deal with them once and for all in order to cleanse them from your energy. This must occur for the cleansing of karma.

5- *Your eating habits will change.* Instinctively you will begin to eat healthy, whole foods which vibrate with your ever increasing vibrations.

6- *Your 6th sense increases.* You may hear voices, see apparitions, or sense a presence. As this happens, you may feel fearful about it. Don't. Instead, protect yourself with white light of the Holy Spirit, then you'll be free to enjoy it! Ask questions and find out whatever it is they want you to know.

7- *You will begin to see the world through loving eyes.* The reality of our oneness with everyone and everything becomes real to you and judgment of others disappears.

8- *Old habits and patterns will fall away.* Anything that is no longer useful to you will have to clear out in order to make room for the new incoming energies.

9- *You'll notice more and more signs.* Little things will speak to you in a profound way because of your growing awareness.

10- *Synchronicity flows faster.* You'll see the pattern in everything, and feel how it all works together in harmony.

Calm Scene Meditation

Get comfortable in your favorite chair, legs uncrossed, feet flat on the floor, hands in your lap, and close your eyes. Breathe deeply and slowly.

Imagine you're stepping into an elevator. The door closes and you will descend three floors. Take a deep breath and feel the relaxation begin. Take another nice, deep breath and descend another floor. One more nice big cleansing breath, and release all stress and tension from your body.

You've reached ground level. You are very deeply relaxed. The elevator doors open and you walk out into a lovely green pasture. There is a shimmering lake in the distance with a big, full, mature weeping willow tree on the shore before it.

To your left is a grove of trees that extends back and surrounds the far side of the lake. Slowly make your way to the weeping willow and feel the soft grass on your feet,… smell the fresh spring air,… the blossoms in the pasture. See the swans glide across the glassy surface of the lake.

You're in paradise,… your own personal Calm Scene. Your loose, comfortable clothing swirls lightly around your ankles in the gentle warm breeze, while the sun kisses your upturned face.

When you reach the majestic willow tree, make your way around to the far side of it so you are between the tree and the lake. Find a comfortable place to sit among the roots,… maybe you can lean back against the tree. Take in the sights and sounds of the lake and the trees,… the birds… the butterflies.

In this beautiful, peaceful, place, you can find the answers to all of your questions. You're completely safe and relaxed, and your senses are alive.

Focus now on opening your third eye and allow messages to flow from Spirit. You may have a question that you need to have answered, or you may simply be open to any messages from Spirit.

When you feel complete, it is time to return to waking consciousness, so begin to slowly make your way back to the elevator. Stand up… feel the warmth of the sun on your skin,… smile,… and breathe in the fresh, spring air. Enter the elevator, and when watch the doors close.

Level one you begin to stretch a little… wiggle your fingers and toes… level two, slowly bring yourself back by breathing deeply,… three, gently blink your eyes open and stretch as if you just woke up.

You are back in the present. Quickly write down the details of the session.

Inner Smile Meditation

This meditation is called the Inner Smile. It is an ancient meditation used by the masters of Tibet.

Let's place our feet flat on the floor, place your hands in your lap, palms up and make circuits with your thumbs and fore fingers. Take a nice deep breath in… and release it. Another nice deep breathe in, and out… One more time, in…. and let it out.

Now let's bring our awareness inside the body and begin to examine the organs one by one. First we'll just look without judgement or preconceived ideas,… get a feel for the condition of each organ, or bodily system,… then we will change our focus to raising their vibrations.

Let's start by examining the head. Begin by looking for pressure or tension behind the eyes,… in the ears,… in the sinuses. Practice sensing the condition of each area as you inhale, and releasing stress you find on the exhale. Once all tension, pain or tightness is gone, bring the high vibration of love into the area on the inhale, and surround it with white light on the exhale.

When these areas of the head are complete, surround the entire head and the brain with love. Imagine your brain, or hypothalamus, creating serotonin,… increasing production of this happy juice to send out into the body. Move your awareness down the brain stem into the spine and throughout the entire Central Nervous System (CNS). Every nerve ending is being cleansed of all tension and sent the frequency of love,… softening and smoothing every connector. Imagine the serotonin molecules landing gently in the cell receptors, then watch as each cell is rejuvenated.

Now we'll move down now to the other organs of the body.

Smile at your heart. Fill it with love. Feel it fill up and just begin to glow. Focus on the veins and arteries and strengthen them… your whole circulatory system… your blood pressure is normalizing…

Examine your liver. Smile and fill it with thanks and love. This is your body's filter and it does a very hard job… thank it for all the work that it does. Cleanse your blood… cholesterol levels are right where they should be… Move on to the gall bladder and do the same. Smile on it and fill it with glorious white light and love. Now go on to the kidneys. Smile at them. Now we'll go on to the pancreas. If you're diabetic, I want you to really focus on sending your pancreas Divine white light and love. Fill it with a sense of perfect health. Imagine your insulin levels normalizing… all of the sugar in your body is being processed perfectly.

Now let's move on to the digestive system…. Feel the length of your intestines glowing with health. Imagine your stomach… the acid in your stomach is perfectly balanced… the right amount of acid to completely digest your food… Lets move down now to the small intestines… the walls of your intestines are pink and healthy… envision the little fingers of the villi lining the intestinal walls as they release all compacted waste and they absorb the nutrients your body needs to free itself of allergies and a multitude of other health issues. Smile on your beautiful, healthy colon… program it to joyfully eliminate all poisons from your system. Fill it with white light and love… If you sense any inconsistencies in the health of your colon or any other organ in the body, this is where you can repair it. Send it glorious white light and love.

Let's move into the joints… any issues with arthritis just melt away… smile on your bones and love them. Release all discomfort. Move into the muscles… feel the love and white light emanating from your heart and going through all of the muscles of your body. Imagine a glow so intense that it flows out of your finger tips and out through your toes.

If you're experiencing issues with any other body part, now is the time to focus on that. Smile on it… love it for doing the job that it does.

Take as much time as you need with this process. Really get into the organs and tissues of your body and you will begin to intuit the health of each part.

You are completely surrounded by this glorious white light… it envelopes you.

When you're ready, you can begin to come back into the room by gently stretching your arms and legs and wiggling your fingers and toes…

You can make yourself well.

Practice this meditation regularly and you will be able to sense the usual vibration of your body, and perceive the differences when things become unbalanced.

Becoming One with Nature Meditation

Close your eyes and send your awareness inside. Feel the vibrations of your Spirit. Imagine the energy that is the real you, flowing through your physical body. Embrace the tingling sensations as they course through and around you. Now surround yourself with white light, then create a protective sheild that surrounds that white light. Pull this shield with your energy in it close to your skin. Now expand it and feel the light filling in the spaces between the molecules of your energy. Feel the lightness and glow as you expand yourself to fill the room… Practice this a few times… Pull your energy in close… feel the warmth and protection… now expand it out…

Imagine your energy expanding and flowing from your body in every direction. Allow it to flow into the floor at your feet. Experience the energy patterns in the tile or carpeting. Allow yourself to become in sync with it. Expand out now to the chair and become one with it. Push yourself out to the walls and become one with the entire structure of the building. Now move out into the grass, flowers, feel the soil and trees growing from that soil, the birds in the branches of these trees, and into the very air that whispers through the limbs. We are the stones, We are the water, We are the asphalt. We are at one with everything around us. We send out love, and We feel love return to us. This is true bliss. We are now the purest form of our beings that we can ever be.

When you walk into a crowded room, feel this energy attracting people to you. It's like a magnet made of the purest form of love and joy, as it courses through us. We attract to ourselves those who would be enlightened, and those who are already thoroughly engaged in their own search for the pathway to real Oneness. This is the Law of Attraction at work. Now, with the introduction of the fifth dimension energies, we can actually feel this phenomenon. It is palpable. We see the colors of auras changing in our midst. They become lighter shades of yellows, blues and violets. Feel the glow of energy from small children and from animals, too.

This energy attracts a great many, but it acts as a repellant to others. There are those among us who are deeply rooted in their ego and in this possession-oriented culture that they want nothing to do with Oneness. You may find that your Spirit makes some people uncomfortable. When we are in tune with this energy it will do us the huge favor of bringing the right people into our lives, and removing the wrong ones from us. A peaceful and harmonious life is within our reach. Stretch out your arms and grab it with both hands. Grab it with your whole Being. Once you do, your life will change in ways you cannot conceive.

Now that you know what it truly is to be one with your surroundings, I'd like you to please come back into the room… gently pull yourself back to this moment… feel yourself in your chair… Take a nice deep breath in… and let it out…

Homework

1. **Daily Meditation**
2. **Nightly Review**
3. **Intuition pair up** – with another student, set an exact time to do this exercise. You will remain in your own homes, as this is an exercise in telepathy.

Instructions: For 10 minutes you will send each other shapes telepathically.

The shapes are **Square, triangle, circle** only!

Decide who is to send first, while the other receives.

PREP: draw 5 shapes in your notebook (They will be any combination of the 3 above).

Leading up to the agreed upon time: ground your energy and clean your chakras.

Right before the agreed upon time: Pair will focus on connecting with each other.

At precisely the agreed upon time: sender will focus on sending the first of 5 shapes. Repeat with the remaining shapes, one minute per shape, for 5 minutes.

For the second 5 minutes, the roles reverse. The sender becomes the receiver.

Suggested Reading:

Buddha, a story of enlightenment, Deepak Chopra

The Immortal, JJ Dewey

Transcendental Meditation, Jack Forem

Anatomy of Energy

Week Three

The Aura and Chakras

Your Aura is the energy field that surrounds your body to protect it from all manner of dis-ease. It is the vehicle our Blessed Higher Self uses to communicate with the subtle energies that surround us and with Spirit.

To 'see' the aura and the chakras, one must open their eyes, *then open them again.*

The difference between the two is the degree of focus. When I look at you casually, I see your physical attributes; hair, skin, clothing, etc., but when I look at someone's energy, I must increase the intensity of my focus. I call that opening my eyes again.

The aura has several layers which correspond with the chakras. A novice can usually see the first, closest layer of the aura quite easily, and the fourth layer not long after, because these are the strongest, and most vibrant.

White light of Protection

To protect yourself when learning this work, you must master this protection technique. You will use it after meditation and before entering into any new situation.

Surrounding your auric field with white light will insure your safety, increase your frequency and attract higher spirit energy during your session.

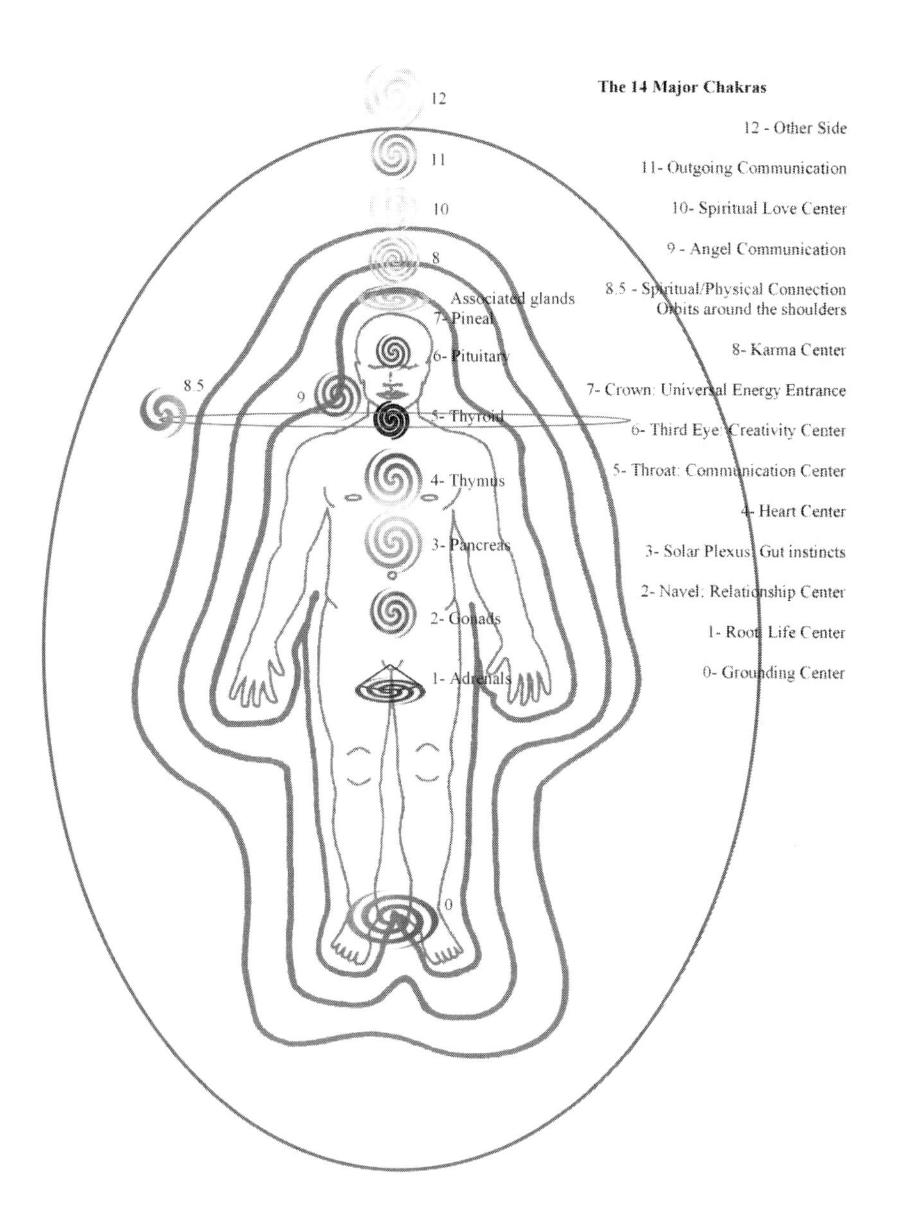
The 14 Major Chakras
12 - Other Side
11- Outgoing Communication
10- Spiritual Love Center
9 - Angel Communication
8.5 - Spiritual/Physical Connection
Orbits around the shoulders
8- Karma Center
7- Crown: Universal Energy Entrance
6- Third Eye: Creativity Center
5- Throat: Communication Center
4- Heart Center
3- Solar Plexus: Gut instincts
2- Navel: Relationship Center
1- Root: Life Center
0- Grounding Center
12
11
10
8
Associated glands
7- Pineal
6- Pituitary
8.5
9
5- Thyroid
4- Thymus
3- Pancreas
2- Gonads
1- Adrenals
0

What is the Aura?

The aura is the part of you that connects your physical body to your BHS. Your personal energy field, or *aura,* has many layers that extend outward from the physical body. This is the real you that remembers Home and all of your other lives. Your Spirit knows why you have chosen to incarnate, and can look objectively at the experiences you have chosen to have this time around. It uses the aura to protect us both physically and energetically. Most importantly, the real you-- your Spirit or BHS-- is a part of God, the Great Spirit, the Universal Source of all things. It is how we connect to, and communicate with God and our guides.

This energy flows through and around you every moment of every day. You breathe it, you hear it, and you see it. We are going to practice becoming aware of this connection, how it can either keep us well, or attract illness. How it picks up on negativity or joy, based on your predispositions (perspective). When you meditate, you will become more aware of *your* energy, and you'll be able to sense the energy of anything that is not you. When this separation is clear to us, we have no need for ego, because we understand that we all are one. This single realization allows us to get our opinionated, emotional selves once and for all, so that the higher frequencies can come through us and get to work.

When you look at yourself in the mirror, you are aware of what you see, but when you close your eyes your awareness goes inside. You can no longer see your body, but there is an inner knowing of something being there.

Exercise 1: Close your eyes and wiggle your fingers. You can feel the muscles and tendons pushing and pulling inside them (Remember the Inner Smile meditation.)

Exercise 2: Stand in front of a mirror and look at your aura. Focus on the space a few inches above your head (make sure there is a white of blank wall behind you). At first you may see only the brightness of it, or you may see faint traces of colors. You may see it the whole time you're looking, or you may only get fleeting glimpses. With practice, your focus will improve.

> **“Every living thing has an aura; every person, animal, plant and bug.”**

Think about that next time you reach out to squash a spider. Instead, look for the energy field around it and know that it is part of the Universal energy that makes us all one. It is a part of you.

Every fruit and every blade of grass has the same energy as you and I. When we are conscious of this, and recognize the life force in a papaya tree, for example, it keeps us from ripping the fruit and leaves from it carelessly. Instead, we learn to approach the tree and communicate with it. Ask the tree which fruit it would like to offer, then when you receive your answer, lovingly thank it for its offering, and gently remove the fruit or leaf.

The animals we eat are to be approached in the very same way. We go into the herd and ask for an offering. The animal will make itself known and then it is our responsibility to see that it is surrounded with love so that it may be gently and reverentially separated from this life.

We understand that all life is precious. No one life is more valuable than any other.

All Are One

What are Chakras?

The chakras are the energy centers of your body. We have 14 major chakras (See diagram on page 51). Chakras 0 through 7 are located on the physical body, and Chakras 8 through 12 are spiritual energy centers only. The first chakra group (zero to seven) are meant to help you with your development in regards to the Earth; and they assist us in communication with our Blessed Higher Selves and our guides; they help us to become one with the planet. Although they have an effect on our health and well-being, they also transmit spiritual energy. The next five, the Spiritual Chakras, (eight to twelve) help us to become one with the universe. Our awareness is slowly being moved away from our Earth center (our own physical selves) and is moving outward to encompass the larger framework of other peoples' realities, and divinity itself. In this way, we become more than we were before and more, clear, refined, and perfect. As we stop focusing on ourselves and begin to focus on these larger energies, we move out of our small world and step into a new Universe where almost anything is possible. From a 'reality creating' standpoint, this shift in possibilities is very, very powerful.

We know that our thoughts create our bodies, and this happens with the help of our chakras. Let's look at the Heart Chakra for instance. It is located on the body, so we feel its energy very strongly. Love is a very specific sensation that emanates from your energy field through the heart chakra. When your heart has been broken it is not something a surgeon can point to on an X-ray and fix. There is no physical part of you that is broken, but the heartache can be very painful, and no drug can make it better. If we don't allow ourselves to properly process the energy of a broken heart, it can manifest physically and cause diagnosable heart problems. However, when we consciously surround ourselves with the highest vibrational frequencies of Universal love, we simply cannot become physically ill.

This is just one example of how we experience life with our chakras. We can feel all of our energy centers-- our major chakras-- albeit to different degrees. It is essential to our health to maintain the flow in our energy field, of which the chakras are a part.

Anatomy of the Chakras

Physical Chakras

Foot Chakra - Zero Chakra

Color: Hunter Green/ Deep Brown

Location: Soles of the feet (although there are two feet, this is considered one chakra)

Physically effects: Mental health.

Energetic activity: Grounding frenetic and nervous energies. Creates balance between the individual and the earth. Relieves anxiety and stress.

Base (Root) – First Chakra

Color: Red

Location: The Perineum, the point between the sexual organs and the anus

Physically effects: Prostate gland (in men) bladder, colon, lymph system, skeletal system, teeth, lower extremities.

Energetic Activity: Maintains the individual's connection to this life.

Navel (Spleen, Sacral) – Second Chakra

Color: Orange/pink

Location: Abdomen

Physically effects: Lumbar plexus, reproductive organs.

Energetic activity: Holds relationship energy. Creates balance between the individual and the people encountered in this life.

Solar Plexus – Third Chakra

Color: Yellow*

Location: Solar Plexus

Physically effects: Large intestines, stomach, liver, muscular system, skin.

Energetic activity: This is where we experience our ‘gut reactions’ and fear. Our ‘fight or flight’ survival instincts live here.

Heart Center– Fourth Chakra

Color: Green*

Location: Center of Chest

Physically effects: Heart, Circulatory System, Lungs, Chest.

Energetic Activity: This is where we experience the incredible love of the Divine, love for others and the loss of love.

Throat - Fifth Chakra

Color: Blue

Location: Throat

Physically effects: Throat, Neck, Arms, Hands. Brachial or Cervical Plexus

Energetic activity: This is where communication occurs. When we choke back, or scream out, our responses, we cause damage in these areas.

Third Eye (Brow) – Sixth Chakra

Color: Indigo

Location: Central Forehead

Physically effects, Temples, Forehead

Energetic activity: the Sixth Sense is experienced through this chakra.

Crown – Seventh Chakra

Color: Violet

Location : Top of the head

Physically effects: The brain, the nervous system

Energetic activity: Gateway for Divine energy to enter the body.

*NOTE: When you can see the third and fourth chakras for yourself, you will notice that the Solar Plexus may look green, and the Heart Chakra may appear to be yellow. This happens when a person is out of balance on the 'love - fear' scale.

Spiritual Chakras

These energy centers do not reside on the body. They communicate complex energies between the body and the Other Side.

Karmic Center - Eighth Chakra

Color: Shimmering Ultraviolet

Location: two feet above the head.

Energetic activity: Stores karmic energy. Past life information can be found here.

Bridge Chakra - Eight and a half Chakra

Color: Shimmering Amber

Location: between 4 and 8 feet from the body, generally orbiting around the head and shoulders.

Energetic activity: Connects the physical and Spiritual Chakras. This is where the energy practitioner makes the connection to the clients BHS, with the assistance of the Amber Angel.

Message Center - Ninth Chakra

Color: Shimmering Magenta

Location: In the angelic realm. However, the energy of this chakra comes to us through a golden horn to the base of the skull.

Energetic activity: Promotes communication with higher energies. This energy center delivers information from the collective unconscious, to the pineal and pituitary glands, as well as to the third eye.

Spiritual Love center - Tenth Chakra

Color: Shimmering Gold

Location: Six feet above the head.

Energetic activity: The Spiritual Love center filters Divine Love from the collective unconscious down to the body.

Prayer Center - Eleventh Chakra

Color: Shimmering Aquamarine/Turquoise

Location: twelve to fifteen feet above the head.

Energetic activity: Communicates our prayers, desires and will out into the collective unconscious to the benefit of all.

Clarity Center - Twelfth Chakra

Color: Shimmering Crystal/Diamond Clear

Location: On the Other Side; Home.

Energetic activity: This energy center connects us to the Divine, our guides, and loved ones; places and things on the Other Side are accessed here. If you ever want to visit the Akashic records, for instance, you will enter through this energy center.

Chakra Clearing for Energetic Healing – Meditation

Should be done when you wake up in the morning to prepare for your day.

Begin to relax and close your eyes. Take three deep, cleansing breaths.

With your mind, visualize the neon hunter green/dark brown spinning wheel of light of the foot chakra, surrounding your feet. Spin it to release any cluttered energy until you feel that it is clear. Think of this as you would the rinse cycle of a washing machine. While the Zero Chakra is spinning, think of strengthening words associated with it: *grounded, balanced, steady.*

You'll know when you're done because you will feel a sense of completion.

Then the Root Chakra will begin to ask for your attention. Imagine this chakra as a neon red spinning wheel of light at the base of your spine. It is your connection to this life. The strengthening attributes for the First Chakra—Root Chakra: *Security-foundation-fidelity.*

Then the Second Chakra begins asking for your attention.

The Second Chakra, the relationship and Health Chakra, appears as a neon pink-orange spinning wheel of light, right above the Root Chakra between the hip bones. Run this orange Chakra through the rinse cycle. While it is spinning think of strengthening words for the second Chakra; *receiving-creativity-desire.*

The Third Chakra begins to appear before you.

The Third Chakra, the Solar plexus, appears as a neon yellow spinning circle of light. It is the largest chakra in the body. This is where we feel our gut feelings, our emotional warning sign.

It is natural to feel uncomfortable while working on cleansing the Third Chakra. This is where we hold our worries and cares. It is our emotional center. This Chakra tells you that you are in the right place; as it spins you're actually releasing feelings of fear and dread. (Before we were civilized, the warning sensations in this energy center were very important. We would sense a predator, get to safety, and the sensation would subside. Now, we tend to hold onto stress in this energy center. A thing we were never designed for.) While it is spinning think of strengthening words for the Third Chakra*; integrity- strength- intention.*

Now, the Fourth Chakra will ask for your attention.

The Fourth Chakra, the Heart Center, appears as a neon green spinning Circle of Light. Focus on the area over your physical heart, and begin the cleansing process. The Heart Chakra generally takes longer to cleanse, but when you're through, you'll feel the warm glow of Universal love come over you.

You can stay at the Heart Center for as long as you like. While it is spinning think of strengthening words for the Heart Center*; Love- peace- harmony- joy- laughter.*

The Fifth Chakra will appear when you're ready.

The Fifth Chakra, the Throat Chakra, appears as a neon blue spinning wheel of light. This is the communication Chakra and it brings you the ability to express yourself. Allow your attention to settle in the center of your throat. Spin and cleanse this chakra until your throat feels clear. While it is spinning, think of strengthening words for this chakra*; compassion- kindness- abundance- affluence.*

Soon you'll see the Sixth Chakra appear.

The Sixth Chakra is your Third Eye. It appears as a neon indigo spinning wheel of light. It is in the center of your forehead, just above the eyebrows. Allow it expand across your vision in an explosion of colors, joining your eyes together as one, opening your awareness wider every time you cleanse it.

As this Chakra spins you become more connected to the Fifth Dimension. The strengthening thoughts for the Third Eye Chakra are *freedom- wisdom- knowledge.*

The Seventh Chakra, the Crown Chakra, appears as a neon violet-white spinning wheel of light. This chakra is located at the top of your head and it can be visualized as a thousand petal lotus blossom. This is your connection to your Blessed Higher Self and Infinity. Envision this lotus blossom opening up on the top of your head. Spin it clear while you imagine a bright light penetrating the center of your head, shining down throughout your body. Strengthening words for the Seventh Chakra are *bliss- infinity- immortality.*

The Eighth Chakra now makes itself known to you as a shimmering ultraviolet wheel of light, hovering two feet above your head. This chakra appears to have a dark center similar in shape to the iris of a cat's eye. As you perceive the light pulsing out from this center, think of the past hurts you would like to release for good, and karmic issues that need to be cleared, whether you are consciously aware of them or not. Be open to receiving past life information in an unemotional manner. Just watch it and let it go. Strengthening thoughts for the eighth chakra are *forgiveness, humility and grace.*

The Eight and a Half Chakra appears now as a shimmering amber wheel of light about 6 feet in front of you. As you spin this energy center, feel the connection to the Divine and concentrate on bridging the distance between this physical world, and the Other Side. Just put out a sense of openness to allow this to occur. Strengthening thoughts for the 8.5 chakra are *connection, oneness and unity.*

The Ninth Chakra calls for your attention. Focus on this shimmering magenta wheel of light at the base of your skull. Now, imagine a golden trumpet, horn or pipeline, at the lips of the Arch-Angel, Gabriel, and the open, receiving end, surrounded by the beautiful magenta glow. Prepare to accept messages from the Angelic Realm. You feel the light of this chakra wrap around your head and shoulders. You may sense a beam of energy move from the base of the skull, up though the pituitary, then the pineal gland, and proceeding outward through the third eye. Spend some time here, open to the messages coming in, and preparing to create whatever you're asked. Strengthening thoughts are *receiving, openness, and connection.*

The Tenth Chakra will beg for your attention when you are ready to move on to its energy. You'll see a shimmering golden ball of light in its position about six feet above your head. The intensity of love that you find there can be overwhelming, but stick with it. Take as much time as you need to acclimate yourself to this new sensation. Spin this chakra clean as you focus on connecting the Spiritual love of the Tenth Chakra to the Heart Center of your Fourth Chakra with an energetic bridge. Strengthening thoughts for the tenth chakra are *Spiritual love and Highest love.*

The Eleventh Chakra makes itself known to you as a shimmering aquamarine/turquoise ball of light, twelve to fifteen feet above your head. As you spin this energy center clean, you will sense it opening, like the petals of a mature rose, reaching out into the collective unconscious which surrounds the earth with all of the prayers and wishes of humanity. Send yours out now as you think thoughts of good will to all. Strengthening thoughts for the eleventh chakra are *good will, peace and empathy.*

When you are through, the Twelfth Chakra will make itself known to you.

It will appear as a shimmering crystal/diamond clear ball of light and you will feel a sense of peace that encompasses all else. Dwell in this peace for as long as you like. Allow your senses to take in the expanse of the Other Side. You may meet your guides here. You may see the Akashic record hall. This is Home and you will be given any messages or insights that you will need to bring back with you to advance your spirit. This is paradise and you will want to come back often. Strengthening thoughts for the twelfth chakra are *clarity, brilliance and pure, unconditional love.*

When you have cleansed the fourteen chakras, take a deep breath, remain silent and still, and surround yourself with white light.

Feel the white light surround your entire body. Feel this Divine light as it expands out to the edges of your aura's field and surround you like you're in an eggshell. Remain quiet with this vision until you are comfortable and feel complete.

Your energy has been cleansed; you are now protected and ready to begin your day.

Working with Higher Frequencies

Now that you are completely blissed out from the chakra meditation, let's come back down to earth for a few pragmatic thoughts, just to keep us grounded.

As you are learning to work with these very high frequencies, keep these things in mind:

- Accept your new abilities and the experiences that come with them.
- Never stop to ask yourself, "What just happened?" Simply allow the information to come through you.
- While you cultivate your Cosmic connection, maintain and continue to develop your will power and integrity. If you should become overly emotional, use the deep breathing and grounding techniques we learned earlier.
- Soaking in a bath, pool or natural body of water is also quite effective if you should feel an excess of frenetic energies.
- While learning, always keep an interest in the physical world. Live in the world and don't look for magic or spiritual experiences in every little thing. Let the growth process occur naturally by keeping up with your meditation practice.
- To remain balanced in this life, be sure to get out and enjoy yourself. Play as much as you meditate, pray and work with these energies.
- Do not take this development so seriously that you can no longer see the humorous side of life. A great shaman is recognized by his or her wit and quickness to laugh, and by the ease with which they experience the world around them.
- Don't allow your ego to get out of control and become judgmental. When this happens, you only set yourself up

for a fall. You are not special; you are one of many and we must work together to heal the world.

- Keep your center. In any crisis situation you are always in control, and when you are in your center, you will react with integrity.
- Do NOT allow flights of fancy to enter your mind before sleep. You are becoming a powerful spiritual being, and it is important to remain grounded.
- Be here 'now'. The present moment is all there really is. Don't forget that.

Connect with your Blessed Higher Self daily by working your chakras, and meditating. This will strengthen your aura and increase your control and focus. Bind your auric field in white light after every meditation and it will become stronger with every session.

Some benefits of raising your energetic frequency are:

- People will no longer be able to lie to you, because you will see and feel the energy that accompanies the words and actions of low integrity.
- You will be able to end conflict with your energy alone. No words will have to be exchanged.
- Acts done in the pure energy of love will be successful, every time.

Having control over these outcomes is what being empowered and enlightened is all about. It is not magic; it is a way of being that can, and should be learned by everyone. This will take the human race to Nirvana.

Homework

1. **Daily Meditation**
2. **Nightly Review**
3. **Practice connecting:** Focus on connecting with a strangers BHS and get info about them. Ex: in a waiting room, store or restaurant. Do not worry about invading their privacy as we all carry very superficial information on the outer layers of our aura. If you find something that makes you feel out of integrity, just stop.*

*Note: We have been working on removing all 'rights' and 'wrongs' in order to realize our oneness. No one way of living is 'better' than any other. Knowledge of our oneness, not our differences, allows us to release the ego. When we release the ego, any interaction we have with another is in Divine order.

The goal of the Empowered Empath/Become your own Shaman class, is to *know*, not believe, that all healing comes from the high Universal vibration of pure love. Period.

Suggested Reading:

The Kybalion, A Study of the Hermetic Philosophy of Ancient Egypt and Greece. Three Initiates

You can Heal Your Life, Louise Hay

Natural Medicine

Week Four

"Let food by thy medicine, and medicine by thy food"

- Hippocrates, the father of medicine

Recap: Weeks one through three

For the first three weeks we focused primarily on our personal energy field, on learning who we are, what our preferences and prejudices are (predisposed ideas), meditation to increase our connection with the Universe, and last week we learned about the bridge between our energetic selves and our physical bodies through the aura and our chakras. When we know ourselves, we can see others clearly and without judgement.

How has your meditation been going? By this point, you should be bursting at the seams with inspiration; stories of incredible insights that you have been receiving from Spirit. You will not get much from the last three classes if you're not connecting.

Remember, in the very beginning I said that I would not be able to teach you anything you didn't already know? I can only help you to access the information you already have within yourself?

We have all been receiving downloads of information since the end of 2012. This energy needs to be assimilated through meditation, to bring us into balance. Otherwise we will have unexplainable bouts of depression, anger, or sadness. Meditation brings us back into balance because it is the only way we can make sense of these new frequencies.

We are becoming programmed with 12 strands of DNA. 4 groups of 3. Scientists have seen it and they are calling it superfluous DNA. They think it's a genetic disorder because they themselves are not connected to Spirit. These new strands of DNA allow us to connect and communicate brilliantly with beings from all over the Universe as well as each other.

The knowledge we gain when we connect regularly allows us the realization that we are complete all by ourselves, and that we do not need another human being to be whole. We are meant to be powerful individuals who come together in harmony. When we have no need of others, we can create from a place of egoless love, knowing that we All Are One.

When we all live at the highest vibration of love, we will see clearly that we have no need of structured religion or government and their reign will be over.

So connect. Resonate with love consciously, at first, then your body will begin to resonate with love sub-consciously. You will be unstoppable! Then share this knowledge with others.

A strong healthy start – Guidelines for Physical Health

The bulk of this course focuses on the mind and spirit but for today we will focus on the basic components of physical health.

Maintain normal weight - Eat fewer calories and higher quality foods. Cut out all of the simple carbohydrates and increase your intake of fiber by eating more vegetables. Remember that no matter the quality of your groceries, it still matters how much you eat. The more you eat, the more activity you will need to add to your routine.

Exercise at least 30 minutes a day - Don't just take a stroll. You need to break a sweat and get your heart rate up. A body in motion tends to stay in motion, and this means that your metabolism, your ability to burn calories, will increase.

Sleep 8 hours every night - Our bodies have a built in sleep cycle. At around nine o'clock in the evening, the chemical melatonin is produced in the brain, which induces sleep. If we stay up later than that, it dissipates and we miss the free sleeping potion and it becomes harder to fall asleep.

We need eight hours of sleep each night, but if we put too much pressure on ourselves to get it, we'll make it hard to fall asleep and stay asleep.

Start a new stress free bedtime routine. Turn off the TV, meditate, journal, have a warm mug of herbal tea, like chamomile. Keep your bedding clean and cozy. Studies have shown that sleeping under a warm heavy comforter eases anxiety. Perhaps that's where the name came from! Before you know it, you'll have established a new sleep schedule and your body will get the new routine. You'll not only get used to it, you'll crave it.

When you consistently sleep eight hours a night your body has the time it needs to heal itself. Not only do the circles under the eyes diminish, but skin gets soft and smooth and hair gets shiny.

Better than these outward signs are the things that go on inside your body. While you sleep, cells repair themselves throughout your entire system: Think about what that means. That's what your body is – a huge structure made up of cells. Fighter cells (T-cells) go out on scouting expeditions and round up the poorly formed and alien cells (cancer cells) as well as the old dead cells before they can do any damage.

Stay hydrated - Water is the life blood of your cells. They can't multiply or remove toxins from the body if they're under nourished. If you tend to retain water, it's because you don't drink enough of it. Your body is very smart and it will hold on to what it has stored if you don't put in a fresh, new supply. Soft drinks, sodas, and coffee are not hydrating. They actually increase your need for water, so avoid them as much as possible.

Maintain Healthy Relationships - When we enjoy the presence of the people we surround ourselves with, stress levels decrease, and serotonin levels increase. Good relationships are built on good communication, mutual respect and tend to have lots of laughs thrown in. Studies have shown that a nice warm hug can melt anxiety away (did we need a study to tell us that?). I recommend 8 doses of Vitamin H, *Healthy, Healing Hugs* a day for optimum health. Hug your spouse, your kids and your friends.

Nurture your physical relationships – The human body was created as a vehicle for our spirit to experience this life to the fullest and a huge part of that is the physical expression of love. Express your sexuality without guilt and without feeling any need to conform to any societal norms. It is vital to physical health that we feel free to honestly and openly express ourselves with our intimate partner(s).

Myth of Treats – We need to change the language we use when we discuss food. When we say that something is *not good for us*, that's obviously not strong enough wording because we eat things that are not good for us all the time. Instead we should say that it's poison because we are literally ruining our health and shortening our lives when we eat imitation food products.

Webster's Dictionary defines poison as:

(1): a substance that through its chemical action usually kills, injures, or impairs an organism: something destructive or harmful. (2): an object of aversion or abhorrence: a substance that inhibits the activity of another substance or the course of a reaction or process.

Isn't that what trans fats are? Sweets? Soft drinks? This word is not restricted to rat bait and cleaning fluids. We poison ourselves regularly and tell ourselves we somehow earned it. "I worked a long shift" or "I ate healthy all week so now I deserve a treat". We poison our children with breakfast cereals, snacks and hot dogs and other things we think of as kid friendly foods.

Our kids are not only heavier than ever before, but they are far less healthy than in previous generations. Studies show that this upcoming generation will have a far lower life expectancy than any generation before. Suggest activities as special treats for the kids. Take them to the park, play a board game, or let them pick out a new book. These things are not only healthier options; they are chances to create lasting memories and strong family bonds.

A treat should be something your whole being can appreciate. Something like a nice soak in the hot tub, or a massage, or even something as simple as a nice cup of tea out on the porch makes a great little gift. Don't allow the reward to be something you'll feel bad about later. That doesn't make any sense.

Generally, you want real food, organic when available, because our bodies understand them. Fewer grains, more animal proteins, healthy fats and lots of veggies is the ideal. a palm sized lean cut of meat, chicken or fish, with steamed mixed greens and root vegetables, all cooked in and/or dressed with essential omega fats (such as extra virgin olive oil, or cold pressed coconut oil) is a perfect dish. Turn the conventional food pyramid upside down with regard to meats and grains.

THE FAULTY FOOD PYRAMID

You're familiar with the standard food pyramid (left), but did you know that it was directly influenced by the *cereal manufacturers*? It stresses loads of carbohydrates and very little protein and natural fats.

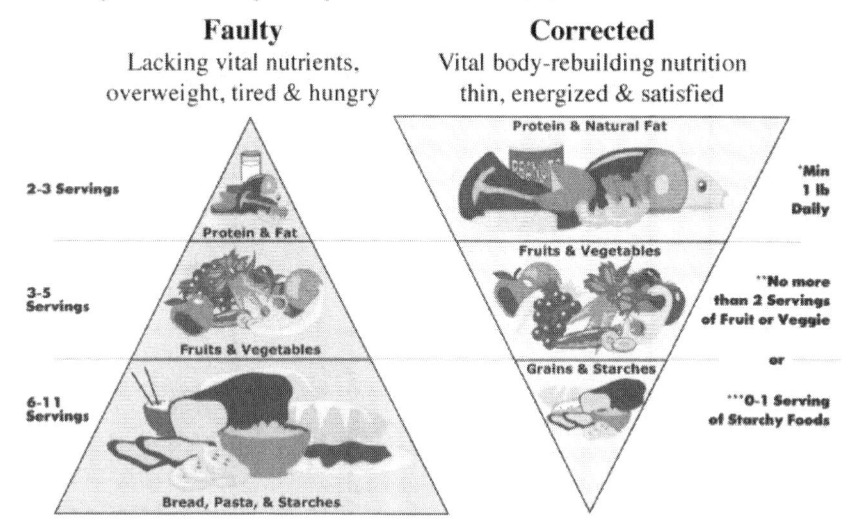

Processed foods represent at least 80 percent of what's available in your neighborhood supermarket, and they are full of chemically-laden food-like substances which contain carcinogenic ingredients, hydrogenated and highly processed oils, MSG and other excitotoxins. They are synthetically fortified and contain little to no nutritional value. We are getting less nutrition and more toxins.

When we eat processed foods, our bodies cannot understand them. Our cells cannot identify the un-natural particles. As a result, our system will try to make use of the foreign, non-food molecules by storing them in places that kind-of-look-like-maybe-it-belongs-here and we wind up with problems like obesity, brain tumors, and cancer.

Let's use aspartame, commonly found in diet foods and soft drinks, as an example. Because aspartame molecules resemble brain cells when viewed under a microscope, when a person consumes aspartame regularly, the body will store this chemical in the brain. As these cells collect, they form a mass that starts out by causing mild headaches, then chronic migraines, and eventually the mass will become a tumor.

However, when we eat real, organic, non-genetically modified (GMO) foods and use natural health and beauty products, our bodies are able to build healthy cells, tissues and organs, increase antibodies and formulate the chemicals our brains need to maintain mental health. Then, our healthy, well-nourished cells are able to remove any foreign (cancer) cells with ease.

We are organic. Our bodies are all natural. Every cell has an energy field, and just like when someone with dark energy enters the room and we feel the energy shift, this same thing happens at the cellular level when an un-natural molecule tries to mingle with the high frequency of our healthy cells. And just like that scenario of a person with dark energy entering a room full of light beings, that energy will be eliminated or asked to leave. But if we continually pollute our body with foods that have dark energy, our defenses weaken, and the dark energy multiplies, creating disease.

The North American idea of health does not work. We cannot scoff at exercise, a diet of real food and a solid meditation practice, and think we can go to the doctor for a pill, or start a juicing plan because Dr. Oz said to, and suddenly become healthy.

When we become serious about changing our lifestyle to create real and lasting health, this shift will come easily and organically. It will seem to ‘just happen’. The more we meditate and focus on raising our frequency, the more desirable real food becomes. We’ll crave it! Old habits will fall away effortlessly.

So change the contents of the kitchen for good.* The whole family will benefit, and you'll all live longer, happier lives.

*Consult with a holistic health practitioner for solid strategies.

History & Guidelines of Herbal Medicine

Humans have been on this planet for thousands of years, and up until about 100-150 years ago we all had healing gardens. If mom burned herself while cooking supper, she would go outside and pick some marigolds, mash them up, and bind them to the wound. We took care of our own health. Around that time, scientists began isolating and synthesizing plant molecules and we started to see the first drugs. Formulas that were patentable and therefore, big money!

The American Medical Association (AMA) was born and they had their "silver bullet" medications. These medications addressed specific symptoms, instead of the whole body, and they wowed everyone, in America that is. Around the world, the importance of using the whole herb is understood to be most effective. In fact, the rest of the world still uses nature to maintain health. You see, herbs work on your whole system, not just one thing. They work to regulate and maintain, without any disruption of healthy functions.

Allopathic Medicine vs Herbal Medicine

Allopathic Medicine is “a system of medical practice that aims to combat disease by use of remedies (as drugs or surgery) producing effects different from or incompatible with those produced by the disease being treated.” [merriam-webster.com]

So we see that the methods used in allopathy include fighting disease and basically going against the illness with powerful weapons. Many medicines used in allopathy use the prefix ‘anti’, as in antibiotic, anti-inflammatory and antibiotic.

Herbal Medicine is a system that seeks to bring the body into balance by supporting systems so that the body can manage the illness with its own healing abilities. There is no fighting involved, rather our intent is to build up the body.

An herbalist understands that the body will always default to health if it is provided with the right ingredients."

The allopathic model of disease and anti-disease medicine is coming to an end, as we see in the case of antibiotics, the more we use them, the less effective they become. The only logical course is to begin to restore the body in the ways that have always worked since the beginning of time. We need to take responsibility and educate ourselves about how a healthy body works. It is time to take our health back into our own hands.

- Herbalism is the oldest system of healing. It has been time tested and approved around the world. AMA is the new kid on the block.
- 82% of the world's population practices herbs as their primary health care tradition.
- Herbal "healing" is illegal in the US. The AMA has claimed many words as their own; heal, and cure along with the word patient, may not be used by a holistic practitioner, so be very careful.

Complete Health Care Model

That said, when we have an illness, there are four experts that we need to consult to get complete care: a doctor, a chiropractor, a holistic practitioner and a spiritual advisor.

First, we need to see a doctor first for a diagnosis. This is the 21st century and we should definitely take advantage of the diagnostic advances available to us, such as blood tests, x-rays and ultrasound imaging.

Then, armed with your diagnosis, go visit the chiropractor for an alignment. Chiropractors have extensive knowledge of anatomy and can bring balance back to the supportive frame of the body.

Next we go to see an herbalist, holistic practitioner or natural health care provider who is well versed in herbs, vitamins and nutrition because we need to know the ingredients that are necessary to restore balance to our bodies on a cellular level.

Lastly, and possibly most importantly, we need to talk to our spiritual advisor, priest, minister or rabbi because all illness is rooted in the spiritual energy system.

Traditionally, the shaman, holy wo/man or medicine wo/man is knowledgeable in the workings of the body, knows how to treat the body with natural medicine, can talk through issues with us like a therapist and is able to converse with the spirit. This is known as the 'holistic' approach because it engages the mind, the body and the spirit of the client. The whole person.

You may fall into one, or more of these categories already, and your knowledge will certainly be broadened once you have completed this course. Based on your particular calling or comfort level, you will decide what to put on your business cards.

Working with herbs in your own home:

- Keep it simple and safe
- Use only organic or carefully wild crafted herbs
- Create a Materia Medica (herbal medicine chest) of your own
- You can use a few herbs for many things. Get to know these amazing plants.
- Get one or two ounces of several herbs, bring them home, put them in glass jars, and give them a place of honor in your home A special cabinet or shelf (out of direct sunlight) is perfect.
- Then start working with them. Use your home remedies for simple ailments

Talk to the herb, and trust the intuitive information you receive:

- When you encounter a new plant that you would like to get to know better, aside from reading up on it, spend some time with it. Become familiar with its vibration and listen to any messages it has for you, then trust what you 'hear'. I have had instances where my knowledge and my instincts did not match, and I will always trust my Spiritual guidance in these situations.

- There are always several herbs to choose from for any given ailment, so if one feels wrong, rest assured that there is another plant which will perform the same task.

Three categories that all herbs fit into:

1- Adaptogenic/tonic herbs: Food herbs, herbs with a long history of use and don't build up in the body. Generally have no harmful side effects. Ex: garlic and dandelion.
2- Medicinal Herbs: Can cross over into tonic herbs category, but peppermint is a good example of an herb that is used as a food and a medicine.
3- Powerful Herbs: Used in pharmaceuticals, rich in alkaloids and glycosides, and have a marked physiological action in the body. Ex: golden seal, coffee and tobacco.

Safety Net – Before taking, or prescribing an herb for someone else, always research your herb in at least 3 herb books (books written by certified Master Herbalists) to insure proper usage. These are some of my favorites:

- *Herb Contraindications and Drug Interactions* by Dr. Francis Brinker
- *Botanical Safety Handbook*, edited by Michael McGuffin, Christopher Hobs, Roy Upton, and Alicia Goldberg
- *Drug-Herb-Vitamin Interactions Bible* by Richard Harkness & Steven Bratman, and *JGI* (Just Google It!)
- Use herbs with a long history of being safe.

You now have a better understanding of the power of natural medicine. Our connection to Mother Earth and the Universe, (Divine Love), will always be the source of all healing.

Materia Medica – My Herbal Friends from Central America

The following is in no way the complete list of rain forest herbs, but they are my favorites, and I use many of them in my Bush Medicine by Blossom Spring® remedies.

Allspice ***(Pimenta diotica)***

A tea made from one leaf to ever cup of water is used for digestive upsets. Sip it all day long. Also effective against diarrhea. This same tea can also be used to treat menstrual cramps. When there is no water available, the leaves can be chewed for their water content. A pain relieving poultice made from the green, unripe berries and leaves, can be applied to the gums for toothaches. An infused oil made of the berries can be used to combat foot fungus. A plaster made of boiled down juice from the berries is used to treat rheumatism when applied to a cotton or wool cloth and bound to the affected area.

Aloe leaf(*Aloe Vera*)

This very useful plant is valued for its ability to treat burns, eczema, psoriasis and open wounds when applied topically and is used internally for detoxification, constipation and other digestive problems. DO NOT eat the leaf because it is poisonous. There are safe juices commercially available. Get Aloe Vera juices at your local health food store. Do not use in cases of Crohn's disease, colitis, or unknown abdominal pain.

Avocado ***(Persea Americana)***

A tea made from the leaves is used for colds, high blood pressure, coughs, fever, diarrhea and menstrual cramps. For acute lung issues, make a tea with avocado and soursop leaves. A tea made with the leaves of avocado and mango is drunk for three days to reduce bruising (one cup, twice daily). For diarrhea make a tea from the bark and drink a cup each day until symptoms ease. The seed is used to treat type II diabetes when mashed and boiled and prepared as a tea. A leaf poultice is used for headache, joint pain and sprains. Do not eat the fruit if you have an open wound as it could impede healing.

Coconut ***(Coco nucifera)***

The water from the young fruit is very nutritious and it is used to treat disorders of the kidneys, heart and liver, as well as toxemia in pregnancy, gonorrhea, and high acidity of the urine. Mature coconut water is used for dehydration, indigestion and can even be mixed with infant formula to prevent colic.

Contribo ***(Aristolochia trilobata)***

A tincture or decoction is used to treat hangovers, flu, colds, sinus congestion, indigestion, colitis, high blood pressure, loss of appetite and scanty menses. This is truly a tonic herb.

Copal ***(Protium copal)***

The bark is used to treat wounds and open sores. The resin is used to treat mouth pain and broken teeth. The resin is also used ceremonially, like an incense, to clear space.

Ginger Root (*Zingiber Officinale)*

Nothing works better for indigestion. I always keep a jar of crystallized ginger root pieces in my kitchen for relief of indigestion of all types. Great for morning sickness and motion sickness as well. Also used for treatment of migraines, rheumatoid arthritis, colds, flu, and menstrual cramps.

Gumbo Limbo ***(Bursera simaruba)***

The only known antidote to the sap of the black poisonwood tree. The bark is used for skin ailments such as sunburn, sores, insect bites, and measles. Taken internally for infections, to purify blood.

Hibiscus ***(Hibiscus rosa-sinensis)***

The red hibiscus is the only variety used medicinally. The flowers are used to treat postpartum hemorrhage, excessive menstrual flow and to prevent miscarriage. The leaves are used to treat menstrual cramps and can also be mashed and applied to the forehead to relieve headaches.

Ix-canan *(Hamelia patens)* *aka Polly Red Head*

Used for skin infections. Anti-fungal as a wash, in a salve or when a powdered, dried leaf is sprinkled on an open wound.

Jackass Bitters *(Neurolaena lobata)*

Treats parasitic conditions of all kinds and it's a powerful fungicide. Also used to bathe stubborn wounds.

Lemongrass *(Cymbopogon citratus)*

Used to treat fevers and colds, as it promotes perspiration and loosens phlegm. Also treats stomach cramps. Lemongrass tea is used as a coffee or tea replacement as it is also stimulant.

Moringa *(Moringa Oleifera)*

Rich in vitamins and minerals, the fresh Moringa leaves are eaten in salads and made into tea. The dried, powdered leaves can be added to any dish or smoothie. Used for diabetes control, relieves diarrhea, aids in childbirth, and treats liver and stomach disorders. It is naturally antibiotic and is used to treat colds.

Oregano *(Lippia graveolens)*

This plant is highly antibacterial and anti-fungal. The oil of oregano can be used topically for skin infections, and taken internally to treat upper respiratory infections and induce or increase menstrual flow.

Papaya *(Carinca papaya)*

The fruit, combined with crushed seeds, can be used to heal wounds, cuts, and infections. The almost rotten fruit is rubbed on the fire coral rash. The juice from the stems is applied to warts and corns to make them dissolve.

A strong tea made from the leaves is used as an antidote for Dengue Fever, a communicable disease, which is passed to humans through mosquito bites.

Wrap tough meat in the leaves for an hour or two to tenderize.

Piss-a-bed ***(Senna alata)***

So named for its ability to treat urinary tract infection. Relieves ailments of the liver, kidneys and lymph system. Also relieves constipation and female fertility problems.

Purslane ***(Portulaca olenacea)***

Crushed stems and flowers are used to stop bleeding and, when applied to forehead, relieve the headache associated with too much sun exposure. Very nourishing, is also cleans the blood.

Rabbit's Paw ***(Sphagneticola trilobata)***

Take internally to relieve infections in the urinary tract, and for liver congestion. Leaves and stems are used topically for pain in the joints, backache, muscle cramps and swelling.

Scoggineal ***(Opuntia cochenillifera)***

This cactus is used to treat headaches and fever, but its power is most impressive as a wound healer by simply placing a peeled pad on the wound.

The fruit is used as a hair conditioner, while the pads can be used in a rinse to prevent hair falling out.

Skunk Root ***(Chicocca alba)***

A tea is used for many digestive disorders and feminine reproductive issues. A wash can be used for sores and rashes.

It is also used to cure alcoholism. When a person wishing to stop drinking consumes alcohol that this root has been soaked in, he will vomit uncontrollably and abhor the smell of alcohol for years!

Tamarind ***(Tamarindus indica)***

Very nutritious. Cleanses the system. Used for morning sickness, sore throat, and can be used as a wound wash. Powder made from the dried leaves is sprinkled on open boils and ulcers.

Tree of Life *(Kalanchoe pinnata)*

Mashed leaves are used to treat headaches, bruises, swelling and cuts. Combined with castor oil (Palma Christa) to make a poultice to relieve mastitis. The leaves are commonly eaten as a panacea.

The Tree of Life is also known as the Life Everlasting" plant because a fallen leaf will take root and become a new plant. This plant is considered sacred for this reason.

Twelve O'clock *(Mimosa pudica)*

Antispasmodic, sedative, and diuretic. Its leaves are dried and smoked for insomnia, nervous irritability and muscle spasm relief.

Vervain *(Stachytarpheta cayennensis)*

A cooling herb that is used as a tea for fever, nervousness, cough, colds, flu and liver and stomach complaints. Cleanses the uterus after childbirth when used as a douche. Clears intestinal parasites when fresh juice is taken.

The Maya hang dried bunches in their doorways to repel evil spirits.

Wild Yam root (*Dioscorea Villosa)*

Used as a treatment for osteoporosis, it is an excellent source of Beta-Carotene and diosgenin, which are powerful phytochemicals which aid in optimal breast development. Wild Yam has been used as birth control. If you are attempting to conceive, this herb could prevent pregnancy.

Planting & Harvesting

Some important rules

Harvest only from an area that is densely populated with the plant you need, and take just enough for your own use.

Choose high quality plants to work with as you cannot improve upon the raw materials.

Do this with love in your heart and peace in your soul. This honors the Spirit of the plant and your end product will be blessed by this intention with which you work.

All of nature, plant life included, is affected by the phases of the moon. When the moon is full, tides are high and the medicinal properties are in the tops of the plant or tree. This is the time to harvest flowers, leaves and fruits. Farmers have always known this. Think of the huge, full, Harvest Moon in the fall to help you remember. Conversely, when the moon is new, all of the plants medicinal properties are in the roots. This is the time to harvest them.

Also, you always want to put new plants in the Earth during the New Moon because they will take root more readily.

When harvesting bark from a live tree, take only what you need. Use a clean, sharp blade, and cut deeply enough to just separate the bark from the outside of the limb. Do not ‘ring’ the tree as you will kill it. Take sections only one-quarter of the way around the limb’s circumference.

If you require more, remove an entire limb and strip it. Generally the outer bark is removed and the inner bark dried for use in your recipes. I like to do this at the three-fourths moon in the fall. In the spring the tree sap is flowing copiously to the limbs to create new leaves and flowers so if you cut into the bark while this is going on, it will bleed out profusely from the smallest incisions.

Muscle Testing a.k.a. Applied Kinesiology

Muscle testing is used to determine whether an herb, vitamin or food is right for you by asking your Blessed Higher Self to provide the answers, instead of your conscious mind. You can have someone test your muscles for you, but since this is a course about personal empowerment, I will teach you how to test your own.

Stand with your feet shoulder width apart, without locking your knees. Keep your neck and shoulders relaxed, and arms hanging loosely by your sides. Now close your eyes.

Use several questions to establish a base line, or in other words, to determine how your Blessed Higher Self communicates to your body, and thus, your conscious mind.

For instance, ask silently, "Is my name (make up a name)?" Pay close attention to the direction your body sways. This is how your BHS says "no".

Now ask questions with "yes" answers, starting with your name. When you are confident in your ability to 'hear' the answers of your Blessed Higher Self, you can begin testing.

Hold a bottle of herbal capsules against your chest in front of your heart and silently ask, "Do I need this?" If you get a no answer, put it down. If you get a yes, continue by asking how many, how often, etc. until you have all the information you need about this one remedy.

Do this when you shop for anything consumable such as food, vitamins, beverages and snacks.

Making Herbal Medicine

Now that we're becoming more familiar with the plants, let's turn our attention to their uses. With your organic, pesticide free herbs, either from your own garden or your local health food store, there are various ways to administer herbal remedies.

First you will determine, either with a doctors diagnosis, your own knowledge, or through muscle testing, what the ailment is that we're addressing.

Methods of Herbal Medicine Delivery

Tea

The simplest way to administer herbs is in a tea. Place the fresh or dried herbs into a glass or ceramic teapot, then add filtered water, which has just come to a boil, to your herbs. Allow them to steep for 5 minutes, then strain. The just boiled water will release the medicinal properties from a leaf or flower and disperse it into the hot water for our consumption. Herbal teas are best when used hot, at room temperature, or iced. Once brewed a tea needs to be refrigerated as it will go bad quickly at room temperature.

For chronic problems, (ie; allergies, arthritis, bronchial problems or other long standing imbalances) a cup of tea should be taken 3-4 times a day, for several weeks. For acute problems, (ie; toothaches, wounds, bleeding and sudden onset of cold or flu symptoms) give 3-4 cups a day, ¼ to ½ cup at a time, until symptoms subside.

Decoction

A decoction is a more vigorous method of water extraction. When your remedy calls for the use of a bark, nut hull, or other heavy dried plant material, it is necessary to simmer them for an hour or so to release their medicine.

Tincture

Tinctures are concentrated remedies which require several weeks to make. It's best to have your favorites on hand for any common ailment. There are alcohol tinctures and glycerin tinctures and even tinctures made with vinegar, but my favorite way to tincture is a combination of alcohol, glycerin and distilled water. The reason for this is each plant has water soluble nutrients, oils, which are better absorbed by glycerin, and more stubborn medicinal properties which are best extracted by alcohol. In this way, I am sure that I have all that the plant(s) has to offer in my tincture. Place your herbs in a jar with a tight fitting lid and cover with your chosen liquid. Place in a sunny window for 2 weeks, shaking and infusing with energetic intention every day.

For chronic problems, ½ to 1 teaspoon of a tincture should be administered 3 times daily. For acute problems, give ¼ to ½ teaspoon every 30-60 minutes until symptoms subside.

<u>Syrup</u>

Made by combining honey with decoctions, a syrup is a very palatable way of administering herbal remedies. Usually used for coughs and sore throats because of their ability to coat and soothe mucus membranes of the esophagus. To combine the honey with your decoction, slowly bring them up to 100-105 degrees F. Stir occasionally for 15 minutes, taking care not to go higher than 110, as this will render the enzymes in your honey useless.

<u>Capsule</u>

An ideal way to administer unpalatable herbs, a capsule is a simple way to get the medicine into the body. Blend the powdered, or ground dried herbs in your blender, then fill empty capsules available online or in your health food store.

For chronic problems, 2 capsules should be administered 3 times daily. For acute problems, give 1 capsule every hour until symptoms subside.

<u>Suppositories</u>

In instances of extreme digestive disorders, or when suffering with damage to the mucus membranes of the lower bowel, a suppository will be your best delivery system. Nutrients CAN be absorbed into the body through the colon when it's impossible to take your herbs orally. Great for babies and small children. Simply grind up your herbs and mix into cocoa butter. Then form into shapes that resemble large tablets, wrap with waxed paper and refrigerate.

Infused Oil

Made either by heating herbs and oils together in a double boiler, or in a cold infusion method (see tinctures), an herbal oil can be used as an addition to massage oil, a salve or a lotion.

Salve (pronounced sav)

When treating a scrape, burn, bite, cut or anything on the skins surface, a salve is the best vehicle for getting herbs into the affected area. A salve is made by combining and herbal oil with beeswax or any oil that becomes solid at room temperature.

Combine 1 ounce of beeswax for every cup of oil for a firm salve.

Lotion

A lotion is typically used for the complexion or for the treatment of dry skin anywhere on the body. It is *not* my favorite method of cosmetic herb delivery because a lotion is mostly waxes. These waxes, although all natural, still clog pores, so it seems to me that applying the oil directly makes more sense. However, when traveling, you may find it difficult to transport oils (they don't always seal nicely in the bottle). A lotion can, however, be tossed into your purse. It takes quite a bit of practice to make a lotion, as it is a water and wax combination that includes an emulsifier to combine the two. This requires just the right mix of ingredients, temperature, and lots of patience.

Keep it Simple - Assignment

For this assignment, our client is presenting with digestive issues, inflammation, vertigo (dizziness), frequent headaches and general fatigue.

Look through your materia medica (there are several suggested herbal reference books at the end of this chapter) for herbs that address the issues you wish to treat, then we'll need to decide upon the best delivery option.

The easiest answer is usually the best, and safest, approach. We want an herb, or combination of herbs, that will address the symptoms. Now we want to administer the remedy in the most efficient manner available to us. Since our client has systemic issues that aren't related to a specific body part, we want to get the medicine inside the body orally.

How will you treat your client? With what herb(s) and which method of delivery?

Homework

4. **Daily Meditation**
5. **Nightly Review**
6. **Make an Herbal Remedy** – Using the information from today's class, make a remedy for our client.
7. **Keep a food diary** – We will do this all week for two reasons. One, so you can see what you normally eat, because sometimes looking back at such a list can be eye opening, and two, to help you make conscious, healthy choices.

Suggested Reading:

The Herbal Medicine Makers Handbook, James Green

It Starts With Food, Dallas and Melissa Hartwig

Herbals:

Heinerman's Encyclopedia of Herbs & Spices, John Heinerman

Natural Health Encyclopedia of Herbal Medicine, Andrew Chevallier

Messages from the Gods, Rosita Arvigo

The Healing Power of Rainforest Herbs, Leslie Taylor

And any others that call out to you

Gifts of the Spirit

Week Five

Your Spiritual Gifts

A test for discerning your purpose in this lifetime

You're about to learn what your Spiritual gifts are. This is why it is so important to know them:

A Spiritual gift is the primary means by which the Universe can work through us.

A Spiritual gift is a supernatural capacity, not an ability.

It's a supernatural desire that is so strong that it may sometimes feel like a burden to you, until you find a way to make use of it.

When you learn what your Spiritual gifts are, they will become an overwhelming source of joy in your life when you are using them.

A Spiritual gift is a Divine motivator which ultimately influences your actions.

It is a Divine calling and responsibility because your individual Spiritual gift is an essential component within the whole of the human oneness.

Answer sheet (Tear out)

Circle the answer that best fits the extent to which you identify with each statement.

WARNING! Do not score based on what you think should be true or hope might be true in the future. Be honest and score on the basis of past experience for a true measure of your Spiritual Gifts.

Answers are: MUCH - 3, SOME - 2, LITTLE - 1, and NOT AT ALL - 0

1. 3 2 1 0	15. 3 2 1 0	29. 3 2 1 0	43. 3 2 1 0	57. 3 2 1 0
2. 3 2 1 0	16. 3 2 1 0	30. 3 2 1 0	44. 3 2 1 0	58. 3 2 1 0
3. 3 2 1 0	17. 3 2 1 0	31. 3 2 1 0	45. 3 2 1 0	59. 3 2 1 0
4. 3 2 1 0	18. 3 2 1 0	32. 3 2 1 0	46. 3 2 1 0	60. 3 2 1 0
5. 3 2 1 0	19. 3 2 1 0	33. 3 2 1 0	47. 3 2 1 0	61. 3 2 1 0
6. 3 2 1 0	20. 3 2 1 0	34. 3 2 1 0	48. 3 2 1 0	62. 3 2 1 0
7. 3 2 1 0	21. 3 2 1 0	35. 3 2 1 0	49. 3 2 1 0	63. 3 2 1 0
8. 3 2 1 0	22. 3 2 1 0	36. 3 2 1 0	50. 3 2 1 0	64. 3 2 1 0
9. 3 2 1 0	23. 3 2 1 0	37. 3 2 1 0	51. 3 2 1 0	65. 3 2 1 0
10. 3 2 1 0	24. 3 2 1 0	38. 3 2 1 0	52. 3 2 1 0	66. 3 2 1 0
11. 3 2 1 0	25. 3 2 1 0	39. 3 2 1 0	53. 3 2 1 0	67. 3 2 1 0
12. 3 2 1 0	26. 3 2 1 0	40. 3 2 1 0	54. 3 2 1 0	68. 3 2 1 0
13. 3 2 1 0	27. 3 2 1 0	41. 3 2 1 0	55. 3 2 1 0	69. 3 2 1 0
14. 3 2 1 0	28. 3 2 1 0	42. 3 2 1 0	56. 3 2 1 0	70. 3 2 1 0

Finding Your Spiritual Gifts

1. I have a desire to speak direct messages from Spirit that will comfort others.

2. People have told me that I have helped them learn Spiritual truths that they could apply in meaningful ways.

3. I have applied Spiritual truth effectively in situations in my own life.

4. Others have told me I have helped them distinguish key and important Spiritual truths.

5. I have verbally encouraged the wavering, the troubled or the discouraged.

6. Others have noticed that I am able to see through phoniness before it is evident to other people.

7. I enjoy spending time nurturing and caring for others.

8. I frequently am able to judge a person's character based upon first impressions.

9. I consistently look for opportunities to build relationships with those who are not especially Spiritual.

10. I have confidence in the Universe's continuing provision and help, even in difficult times.

11. I give to Spiritual causes so that more people will have the opportunity to become enlightened.

12. I enjoy doing routine tasks that support projects which further the enlightenment of humanity.

13. I receive information that I did not acquire through natural means.

14. I can spend time in study knowing that presenting Universal truths

will make a difference in the lives of people.

15. I can see through phoniness or deceit before it is evident to others.

16. I give hope to others by directing them to Spiritual writings.

17. I believe that the Universe will help me to accomplish great things.

18. I manage my money well in order to free more of it for giving.

19. I willingly take on a variety of odd jobs to allow others time for their Spiritual growth.

20. I am committed, and schedule blocks of time for reading and studying Spiritual writings, to understand the Universe fully and accurately.

21. I pay close attention to the words, phrases, and meaning of those who teach.

22. I invite people to seek their own Universal connection.

23. I reassure those who need to take courageous action in their faith, family, or life.

24. I am challenged to limit my lifestyle in order to give away a part of my income to those who spread Spiritual awareness.

25. I see Spiritual significance in doing practical tasks.

26. I have insight or just know something to be true.

27. I have great compassion for people who are hurting or suffering.

28. I can anticipate the likely consequences of an individual's or a group's actions.

29. I openly tell people that I am a Spiritual person and want them to ask me about enlightenment.

30. I am convinced of Spirit's daily presence and action in my life.

31. I like knowing that my financial support makes a real difference to the outcome of Spiritual projects.

32. I like to find small things that need to be done and often do them without being asked.

33. I have suddenly known some things about others, but did not know how I knew them.

34. I can look beyond a person's handicaps or problems to see a life that matters to Spirit.

35. I give practical advice to help others through complicated situations.

36. I like motivating others to take steps for Spiritual growth.

37. I regularly challenge others to trust in the Universe.

38. I feel comfortable being a helper; assisting others to do their job more effectively.

39. I have discovered important Universal truths through meditation that have benefited others.

40. I enjoy bringing hope and joy to people living in difficult circumstances.

41. I can gently restore wandering souls to faith in their Blessed Higher Selves.

42. I can visualize a coming event, anticipate potential problems, and develop backup plans.

43. I am able to challenge others on the Spiritual path in order to foster Spiritual growth.

44. I believe I have been given an abundance of resources so that I may give more to organizations that increase Spiritual awareness.

45. I readily and happily use my natural or learned skills to help wherever needed.

46. I confidently share my knowledge and insights with others.

47. I enjoy doing practical things for others who are in need.

48. I enjoy cliently but firmly nurturing others in their development on the Spiritual path.

49. I set goals and manage people and resources effectively to accomplish them.

50. I live with confidence because I know that the Universe works daily in my life.

51. I feel compelled to support missions with my money and time.

52. I recognize cultural trends, teachings, or events which contradict Universal principles.

53. I try to have a loving attitude and let others know that I care about them.

54. I feel the need to protect others from doing the wrong things so they can grow stronger on their Spiritual path.

55. When others misuse Spirituality, or misinterpret messages from Spirit, I get upset.

56. Others have told me that my prayers for them have been answered in tangible ways.

57. I sometimes feel that I know exactly what the Universe wants me to do in a specific situation.

58. Studying and sharing my Spiritual insights with others is very satisfying for me.

59. I have felt an unusual Spiritual presence and felt confidence in information I have received, when important decisions need to be made.

60. I have the ability to discover new truths for myself through reading or observing situations.

61. I have urged others to seek Spiritual solutions to their affliction or suffering.

62. I can tell when someone who is sharing a Spiritual message is genuine.

63. I would enjoy spending time with a lonely, shut-in person.

64. Others have told me that I am a person of unusual vision, and I agree.

65. When I am in charge, things seem to run smoothly.

66. I have been able to restore health to the diseased.

67. When I pray for the sick, either they or I have felt sensations of warmth or tingling.

68. When I bring forward a message from Spirit, I believe it is beneficial to all of humanity.

69. I have interpreted Universal messages given to others directly from Spirit.

70. When I pray and meditate, Spirit constantly speaks to me, and I recognize its Universal truth.

Scoring

Total your answers by adding up the numbers in each horizontal row. Write numbers in the margin after each row.

Line this answer key up with your totals to determine your Spiritual Gifts.

A. Prophesy

B. Teaching

C. Wisdom

D. Knowledge

E. Exhortation

F. Discernment

G. Mercy

H. Faith

I. Leadership

J. Miracles

K. Healing

L. Channeling

M. Interpretation

N. Intercession

Definitions of Spiritual Gifts

A. **Prophesy:** The gift of prophesy is the special ability to receive information from Spirit for a Divine purpose.
B. **Teaching:** The gift of teaching is the special ability to communicate information relevant to the health and ministry of others.
C. **Wisdom:** The gift of wisdom is the special ability to know the mind or purpose of the Universal Spirit in such a way as to receive insight into how given knowledge may best be applied to specific Spiritual needs.
D. **Knowledge:** The gift of knowledge is the special ability to discover, accumulate, analyze and clarify information and ideas which are pertinent to the well-being of others.
E. **Exhortation:** The gift of exhortation is the special ability to administer words of comfort, consolation, encouragement and counsel to others in such a way that they feel helped and healed.
F. **Discernment:** The gift of discernment is the special ability to know with assurance whether certain behavior purported to be of Spirit is in reality Divine or human.
G. **Mercy:** The gift of mercy is the special ability to feel genuine empathy and compassion for individuals who suffer distressing physical, mental or emotional problems, and to translate that compassion into cheerfully done deeds which reflect the Universal love of Spirit and alleviate suffering.
H. **Faith:** The gift of faith is the special ability to discern with extraordinary confidence the will and purposes of Spirit.
I. **Leadership:** The gift of leadership is the special ability to set goals for the future and to communicate these goals to others in such a way that they voluntarily and harmoniously work together to accomplish goals that glorify Universal Spirit.

J. **Miracles:** The gift of miracles is the special ability to serve as a human intermediary of Spirit to perform acts that are perceived by others to have altered the ordinary course of nature.

K. **Healing:** The gift of healing is the special ability to serve as a human intermediary of Spirit to cure illness and restore health apart from the use of natural means.

L. **Channeling:** The gift of channeling is the special ability to communicate an immediate message from Spirit, sometimes in a language that they have never learned, that is beneficial to all.

M. **Interpretation:** The gift of interpretation is the special ability to make known the messages of one who channels information.

N. **Intercession:** The gift of intersession is the special ability to pray and meditate for unusual amounts of time on a regular basis and see frequent and specific answers to their prayers, to a degree much greater than that which is expected of an average person.

Assimilating your Spiritual gifts into your daily life

Using the results of the answer sheet, enter below in the "Dominant" section your three highest-rated gifts. Then enter in the "subordinate" section the next three highest scoring gifts. This will give you a tentative evaluation of where your gifts lie.

Dominant: 1. ______________________________

2. ______________________________

3. ______________________________

Subordinate: 4. ______________________________

5. ______________________________

6. ______________________________

What gifts are you currently using in your daily life?

____

____

____

____

Which of these gifts are you *not* especially gifted for? List your lowest rated gifts below:

____

____

____

____

____

Is your job or career using your highest rated gifts? Y / N

In light of your gift cluster, what possible career choices and/or volunteering opportunities may suit you best?

____

Reading Guidelines

Now that we know what our actual gifts are, we can begin to talk about the nuts and bolts of an actual energy reading.

Our main purpose is to increase the client's vibration to bring healing to the body, mind and spirit. To do this we must avoid all conflicts.

Specific Elements of Readings

1. Get your own mind out of the way. Begin with no preconceived ideas.
2. Formulate a question, silently or aloud.
3. With complete faith, say, "I'm ready for your answer"
4. Have the courage to accept, and repeat those answers with no editing or judgement.

The Debriefing- discussion of your findings

1. When talking to people about their belief system or their diet, always use "I" statements. You could undo all the work you just did by saying things like, "You should" or "You shouldn't"
2. Watch your body language. Be open and make good solid, but not creepy, eye contact.
3. Deliver all news of illness in the past tense, because you cleared everything you found.

Note: You are enough. You have everything within you to do a complete, concise reading for your client. You don't need crystals, bells, incense or any other thing. You *may* use them if you like, but you should never go into a situation and think you can't do a reading because you left your tiger's eye at home.

Homework

1. **Daily Meditation**
2. **Nightly Review**
3. **Scenario Essays -** On a separate sheet of paper, use everything you have learned and all that you know about your personal gifts, to answer the following essay questions.

A. You have just 'seen' a serious accident during a reading for a client. You saw the car, the intersection and the other people involved. What do you do?
B. At a gathering, one of your friends suddenly becomes very emotional. There was alcohol involved, and the friend's actions are irrational. What do you do?
C. A very good friend of yours is in a terrible relationship and she tells you her good news; she just got engaged. What do you do?

Suggested Reading:

Hands of Light, Barbara Brennan

Anatomy books, (any)

Clearing Karma

Hypnosis & Past Life Regressions

-

Week Six

I have been a seeker
and I still am,
but I stopped asking
the books and the stars.
I started listening to
the teaching of my Soul.

- Rumi

Being an Energy Healer

What is a healer? Curing and healing are very different. To cure is to erase symptoms. To heal is to assure a state of wholeness. A person *is* whole whether he is missing a limb, suffering from the flu or dying. A healer is someone who recognizes that all healing comes from within, and helps the client realize his inherent wholeness.

Being a healer involves following a code of honor, one that promotes healthy feelings, actions, and beliefs in the client, without compromising the same within the healer. Being a healer involves being wise and acting wisely. Being an *energy healer*, however, involves an understanding of energy and its effects. Being a *subtle energy healer* requires comprehending an even more unique set of issues, as we are interfacing with the subconscious mind, or BHS, of each client.

Let's start with the Hippocratic Oath:

To benefit the sick according to one's ability- Treat only those you are qualified to treat. As an energy healer, you are not qualified to tell a cancer client whether or not he would benefit from chemotherapy.

Keep them from harm and injustice, or tell them if you think they are injuring themselves or someone else- Report an case of abuse or endangerment to the authorities

Hold him who taught me as equal to my parents- Respect your teachers and seek out respectable teachers, trainers and schools.

Do not give a deadly drug to anyone who has asked for it, or make a suggestion to this effect- all energy, herbs, vitamins, light and words are medicines that have an effect on a client. No medicine should be used without full knowledge of its effects.

In purity and holiness I will guard my art- This means your life and your integrity are important, and should not be sacrificed for your work.

Whatever houses I may visit, I will come for the benefit of the sick, remaining free of all intentional injustice, of all mischief, and in

particular of sexual relations with both female and male persons, be they free or slaves- Do not get involved with clients. Most medical professionals cannot date or see their clients outside of work unless treatment has ceased for at least two years.

What I may see or hear in the course of the treatment or even outside of the treatment in regard to the life of men, which on no account one must spread abroad, I will keep to myself, holding such things shameful to be spoken about- We will observe doctor/client confidentiality and all privileges of such. It is vital to have the trust of your client to facilitate the complete sharing of energy. Clients deserve privacy.

A modern version of the oath also recommends avoiding doing that which other specialists can do better. A professional sends clients to the correct referrals.

The Subtle Energy Healer adds the following:

- An energy healer must be knowledgeable about subtle energies and the energy anatomy.
- Understand the relationship between the subtle energy and the physical body.
- Have an understanding of the mental, emotional, and spiritual parts of a person.
- Be attuned to and develop the intuitive aspect of the energy healing art.
- Rely upon intellect and common sense to back up intuitive information.
- Keep informed, read books, and take classes to stay abreast of the latest findings in your field.

Waiver of liability and State Documents

Find out the laws in your state and keep pristine records. Have your clients sign all documentation required by the governing body of your state and keep a waiver as well. This is something I simply like to keep in my file as it contains pertinent information about my clients.

The Power of Your Belief in Yourself

Your effectiveness will depend on several factors. Do you believe in the effectiveness of your chosen healing modality? Do you believe in yourself? Do you believe in your clients' ability to heal? Are you a healer because you want to be of service to others or are you doing it just for the money?

Your energy field interacts with the energy field of your client, so what you believe about yourself and your art, will transfer from your energy field to theirs. Your confidence, knowledge, and with practice, wisdom, will assure your client of your abilities. To generate positive outcomes for a client, a practitioner must hold positive feelings in his or her own heart center, along with the knowledge that we all are one.

As you work with your client, you are really bringing healing to a part of yourself."

Strive to understand the oneness of all things, and send love and light to everyone with the ultimate goal of bringing the whole world into harmony and balance.

With this in mind, it is important to remember that the Universe requires an equal exchange of energy. We cannot receive unless we give and neither can your client. This is a very important point to always keep in mind because although we may want to give healing to others as a gift, it cannot be received without some form of exchange. You are not doing your client a favor if they don't pay you because in the eye of the receiver, what you give away has no worth, but what they pay for has great value. It's the same with giving advice; when you give your advice it is usually not heeded, but if someone makes an appointment, shows up and pays you for your time, suddenly that paradigm makes your advice valuable to someone.

After the price is set and you're ready to proceed, there is another energetic law that you will encounter: A person cannot receive, vibrationally, something that s/he is not a vibrational match to. To facilitate healing, we must raise our vibration to the highest level of love or peace that we want to have, or share, with others. We will learn more about this dynamic later.

****

We all have intuitive abilities, and an energy healer uses intuition to a great extent in his work. Determine which of your intuitive gifts is the strongest, as this will help you to gain confidence in yourself and your work.

- **Kinesiology:** Can be used by anyone with or without confidence in their abilities. You will get answers from your clients Blessed Higher Self.
- **Empathy:** Sensing the emotions, needs and physical conditions of another. The ability to detect smells, feelings, sensations, and body language.
- **Clairvoyance:** Perception of images, Spirits, visions, or colors. Reading the aura.
- **Clairaudience:** Hearing information from the Spirit realm.
- **Clairsentience:** Gaining knowledge instantaneously, with no known source. You suddenly *know*.
- **Distant Healing:** Ability to connect with the energy, or Blessed Higher Self of a client that cannot physically be with you.

Working your chakras to develop your intuition

This is the easiest and most reliable method of increasing your psychic awareness. Do a chakra meditation every day, and sit in quiet meditation to receive information from Spirit. You will find that your connection to Spirit will become stronger with time, and you will be able to connect to Spirit to glean new information faster, and without ceremony.

Gain a good working knowledge of the human body

Read and study about the physical body and the systems that sustain us. When you perceive something is amiss with a squiggly thing in the abdomen, it will serve you to know that this is the spleen, and what the spleens job is. Learn about cells, nerves, tissues, muscles, organs, the circulatory system, the digestive system, the endocrine system, the reproductive systems, the immune system, the lymphatic system, the respiratory system, the skeleton, the skin, the senses, and the brain.

Clearing Karma

What is Karma?

Karma is a term used to describe the energy that we create and carry with us throughout our lifetimes. It is not good or bad, it is simply the collected experiences of the soul. We are expected to make mistakes, then learn from them and move on to the next lesson.

This is the whole point and purpose of life!

When someone is struggling and can't seem to get out of that energy, we use tools like these to clear karma:

- *Hypnosis*- In a trance-like state an individual is led by the voice of another to the point of origin of their problem, in an effort to examine the root cause and release it. New information is then introduced to create a new thought pattern to replace an old one. Great for releasing habits that hold us back, ex: to quit smoking.
- *Past Life Regression*- In a trance-like state an individual is led by the voice of another to the point of origin of the problem, in an effort to examine the root cause to release it. Past life memories alone bring clarity to issues that cannot be explained in a traditional therapy setting. Great for uncovering unexplainable issues such as phobias, relationship problems and to explain why patterns seem to repeat for certain individuals.
- *Shamanic Healing Energy*- In a meditative state an individual's energy is cleared by another both physically and psychically. Indicated for determining energetic roots to issues that a client may, or may not, be consciously aware of. A SHE session alone can address and release old habits, past life issues as well as physical disease. Great for general feelings of unrest or disease without obvious cause.

When facilitating any of these karma clearing techniques, it is of vital importance to be clear yourself. Work your chakras, and have perfect knowledge of where your energy ends and the energy of another begins.

When the emotions of the practitioner get confused with the emotional state of the client, great damage can be done."

Clear yourself of all preconceptions about what you think might be wrong, and be open to whatever comes through, without judgement of any kind. Then, because you are highly intuitive, you will be able to 'follow' your client on their journey. While you are on this adventure with them, you will see what they see, and because you are the non-emotional, uninvolved healer, you will be able to recognize the things your client needs to see in order to clear their issue and lead them to see it themselves.

Example: You have a client with mother issues. You ask your client to go to the *point of origin* of this issue. When you get to this point, your client tells you that she is on the Other Side with her best friend and they are having a great time together. Everything is beautiful. You ask, "Who is that person to you in this lifetime? You see for yourself that her best friend starts to laugh uncontrollably! So you ask her, "Why is she laughing?" Then your client starts laughing, too and says, "Because she *is* my mother in this life! We planned this lesson for each other!"

Can you see how knowing something like this can completely diffuse all of the negative energy between these two people? Now that the daughter understands that she chose this for herself and that her mother is not evil, she can begin to understand that her mother is actually her best friend who agreed to help her learn a lesson for the advancement of her soul.

These are the types of things you will see and clear in order to correct life-long issues for your clients. In this example, I saw that the best friend was her mother in this life, but I could not tell her that. She would never have believed me. Instead, I had to ask her to tell me who she was. The power of past life regressions lies in the client seeing things for themselves.

This is a big responsibility, but with practice, past life regressions can become a very powerful tool in your healing practice.

Regressions

Doing a past life regression is very much like leading a guided meditation. You begin by guiding the client through slow, deep breaths and open up the heart chakra then, instead of describing a scene for your client to follow you through, you give prompts. For instance, you'll ask the client to describe a recent memory. Encourage him or her to give as much detail as possible about their surroundings (sights, smells, sounds, emotions evoked, people involved, etc.) Once they have completely described the occasion, move back in time to an early childhood memory and have them again describe it with as much detail as possible.

Then you take them back into the womb and have them describe any feelings or sensations. From here you lead them backwards to the time preceding their incarnation into this life. Remind the client that they are Home. It is perfectly safe. It is where we come from and where we will return to.

Now, the purpose of past life regression is not to find out if we were once Cleopatra. The whole point of this exercise is to reach back to the point of a specific issue in order to diffuse it and remove its power or pain. So say for instance that your client has an irrational fear of water.

What you'll do is ask him or her to go back to the lifetime that contains the root of the issue. You will ask leading questions such as, "How old are you? What sex are you? Where are you? Inside? Outside?" and most importantly, "Who are you with?" and "Who is that person to you in your current life?"

While you are asking these questions, because your sensitivity has become highly refined over these past weeks, you will be able to see or sense many of the details for yourself. It is vitally important that you NOT tell your client anything that you see! Instead, you will encourage them to see everything for themselves.

When you feel complete and the point of pain has been exposed, gently return to the room and discuss the session and encourage your client to write down anything they don't want to forget that they might not have said out loud.

Please read the suggested reading selection at the end of this chapter for a broader understanding of these principals and the importance of the practitioners integrity during these sessions.

Homework

1. Daily Meditation

2. Nightly Review

3. Write your paper/thesis - what does being your own shaman mean to you? Have I accomplished my goal of challenging your perceptions about reality? Do you have a newfound sense of empowerment? I want you to tell me the impact this course has had, and will have on your future decisions.

Suggested Reading:

Hypnosis Dictionary and Scripts, Dr. Shelly Stockwell Nicholas

Energy Medicine

Week Seven

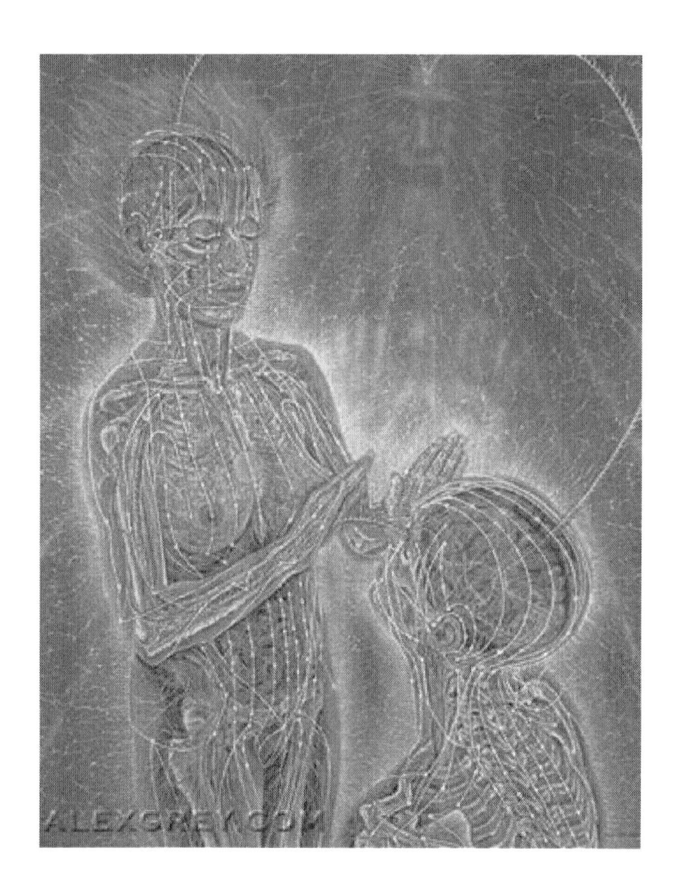

Shamanic Healing Energy™

Training Manual

Shamanic Healing Energy™ (SHE) cannot be learned from this guide alone. Facilitating the enclosed techniques requires hands on training from a certified SHE instructor.

This manual reflects the personal experience of the author. No medical claims are made as to the outcome of this treatment. Each client is encouraged to be responsible in the use and choice of their professional healing assistance as needed.

How Shamanic Healing Energy came to be

In my years as an energy healer, I have studied many methods from around the globe, and found each of them to be, on their own, lacking. Every energy healing modality has its own method, or structure, which is incomplete in that they do not include the healer.

Shamanic Healing Energy™ sessions combine all of the knowledge I have gathered from each method I've learned, as well as the information I have received directly from Spirit, for complete energy clearing in order to facilitate healing.

In 2010, I spent a miraculous weekend with Amritanandamayi, also known as Amma, the hugging saint. She is known for her amazing capacity to love. Of the Hindu concept that all suffering is due to ones actions performed in the past, she says, "If it is one man's karma to suffer, isn't it our dharma (duty) to help ease his suffering and pain?" Amma travels the globe spreading her message of this dharma and she embraces the world. (see www.amma.org for more info) She tells us that "Where there is true love, everything is effortless."

When I saw her at that retreat in Washington D.C., I asked if she would please add her blessing to my healings. She looked me straight in the eye (which is rare) and she took my hands in hers. I could feel the love radiating from her and surrounding me, but through an interpreter she said, "No". She told me that all healing comes from Heaven alone, and that I should go out and heal the world in Heavens name.

Then she gave me her blessing anyway.

From that time to this, I have felt her energy in my healing sessions and I feel her loving embrace when I meditate and pray. She is with me when I am struggling, and she is with me when I am steeped in gratitude. This connection to Spirit is what I intend to impart to you, my student, through this course.

Overview

All disease, let me repeat that; ALL DISEASE, can be healed in a matter of minutes. Volumes have been written about this fact, religions have been formed around it, and I've taken you through seven weeks of training to get to this, the big answer: "You Can Make Yourself Well"

It's so simple, yet it has to take time and effort for our minds to be prepared to grasp it. If I simply told you on day one that you can make yourself well in a matter of minutes, none of you would have come back for the second class.

Everyone is unique, and we each come from a very unique and personal perspective. Dropping all of our preconceived ideas, or at least recognizing them and resisting the urge to let them effect our dealings with others, is the key the being able to use this healing modality.

There is no such thing as a 'typical' session. The process changes based on the needs of each client, and the messages that come through, so the most important attribute a healer must possess is the ability to listen. With my help, you will become a clear channel for Spirit to work through you.

It does not matter if the patient believes in energy therapy because the healer is not communicating with their conscious mind. The healer communicates with their subconscious mind, or Blessed Higher Self, to clear energetic blocks to wholeness."

For many generations, cultures around the globe have practiced some form of energy therapy, each using different names and different methods. All of which have a singular goal; to balance the 'chi' or life force that inhabits each of us. Our energy pathways, or meridians, can become unbalanced and blocked in a myriad of ways. Physical trauma, emotional issues, and even karma from the past can cause these imbalances, and many of us aren't even aware of them. In indigenous cultures it has always been the shaman who sees, and restores, these imbalances.

You will learn to be a highly sensitive, clear channel for this healing energy, and as such, it is important to know that you *will not* take on the energy of your client.

An empath needs to understand a very important distinction:

There are two different types of sensitive people. The first is a noun, meaning a person who is able to sense the energy that emanates from others. The second is an adjective that means a person who is emotional and easily effected by the words and actions of others.

An empath can be both but it is my hope that you have a pretty firm grasp on who you are by this point in your training, and are able to see the distinction between who you are, where your energy ends and where the energy, emotions and issues of another person begins. You are in control and empowered!

As we work with clients we may feel sensations such as tingling and warmth, and we will perceive their emotions as well. It is vital to feel these things, record them, and then move on to the next issue Spirit directs you to. With each session, you will become more and more comfortable with these passing sensations, and your ability not only to perceive them, but your ability to let them pass will improve as well. This is the separation of sensation and emotion; the difference between being sensitive and being emotional.

The Shamanic Healing Energy Session

<u>Prepping yourself for a SHE session</u>

Cleanse your body.

Meditate and cleanse your chakras so that you are a clear channel for the energies to work through.

Claim your Power! Stand firm in your ability to be a clear channel. Remember that you are not a healer, but rather you are an antenna for Universal healing to come through. If you feel inadequate about your intuitive abilities, your client will sense that and close up to you, so don't forget that when you are reaching out to help another from the purest place of love, and your intent is entirely free of ego, the information you need will rush forward. Also, the more healing sessions you facilitate, and the more grounded and relaxed you will become while working, the more intuitive you are likely to become.

Wear comfortable clothing that is light in color and makes no sound when you move. Cotton is best. If you wear long sleeves, make certain that they are form fitting so as not to brush against your client during the session. Remove your shoes. This work is done either barefoot or in stocking feet.

Another word about clothing: For far too long we holistic practitioners have been seen as hippy-dippy weirdos and if we continue to dress in tie died t-shirts and wear patchouli, we'll never be taken seriously. Comb your hair, shower, shave and dress like a professional then you will be treated like a professional.

Do not wear perfume or any strong scents (shampoos, deodorant, etc.), but you must be clean.

Prepping the healing room

These sessions are done with your client in a meditative state so everything we do during the session must be completely silent.

Turn off your cell phone and the ringer on any other nearby phone. If the heater makes noise, turn it off. Same with AC units. If you're in an area where there are going to be sound disturbances that you cannot control, use a white noise machine or run a fan.

I like to have Angels in and around the room and a photo of Amma. Place objects in your healing room that reflect your sources of strength.

Have tissues handy as these sessions can be quite emotional.

Have clean, fresh linens on your massage table.

Have Ardas, or other soothing, high energy music that runs at least half an hour. No drums!!

Have a clock in the room to keep your session to the length your client asked for. Do not go over without prior permission! Respect your client's time.

Have your clip board ready with a waiver and a debriefing form for you to take your notes on, along with a quiet pen. You don't want your client to hear you scratching your notes onto the page or clicking the point in and out.

Have a notebook nearby to write down personal things that occur to you that would distract you from the session if you couldn't get them out of your head. I almost always think of something I need to do later for myself or my family while I'm working, but the moment I write it down, I give myself permission to forget it, which allows me to refocus on my client.

<u>Other options you may choose for your SHE sessions:</u>

Light unscented candles.

Have sage ready in case you want it for clearing strong influences that may surround your client. Use your candle flame to light the smudge to avoid breaking the silence with a match or flick of a lighter.

Have a clear, quartz crystal handy for clearing deeply rooted energy blockages.

<u>Space Clearing</u>

To clear residual energy from your healing space, such as energy from your last client or any negativity that your client may have brought in with them or expressed to you before beginning the session, I find it helpful to draw a clear cut line in the 'before' energy and the 'after' energy which is clean and clear.

I use Into the Mystic™ Holy Anointing Oil room clearing spray or bells to create a clear energetic slate to start the session with.

Spray: Use this once, at the start of your session, with your clients permission and awareness of its purpose.

or

Bells: Have space clearing bells ready in case they are sensitive to scents.

Prepping the client

To avoid any conscious influences in your session, try to learn as little as possible about your client and the reason they came to see you. Advise them that Spirit will tell you everything you need to know and that everything you see will be discussed afterwards.

Let your client know how long the session will last, and ask them if they need to use the restroom before you begin.

Prepare your client by showing them a picture of an energy healer at work. Explain that you will be conversing with their Blessed Higher Self, and that nothing will be done without permission from the BHS.

Start (or re-start) Ardas, or other high energy healing music, then have your client lay face up on the massage table.

Explain that you would like to clear the energy in the room with the space clearing spray. Explain that it is a subtle lavender-sandalwood mixture and that it contains holy water from Amma. If your client has an aversion to scents, use bells to clear the energy.

Have them take three deep, cleansing breaths with you. Advise them to drift without any specific thoughts or prayers; to focus on their breath and on opening their own heart chakra to raise their vibration. We want them to attain a meditative state in which they may receive information from spirit as well.

Tell them that when the session is over you will touch their shoulder 'like this', then touch their shoulder lightly. Let the client know that this is the only touch they will receive from you. That everything you do will take place in the space around and above their body.

At this point I usually give my client a minute to relax into the energies and I fill out the top portion of the Debriefing form.

Connecting to the Blessed Higher Self

This is, and will always be, a Spirit lead healing modality with no real method, per se. However in the beginning, you may feel more comfortable with a few routines that will help you become accustomed to the energy.

Position yourself three or four feet from the crown, raise your arms to ask permission to facilitate healing from your clients BHS, and your guides. Once this connection is established, allow the unconditional love that the Universe has entrusted you with, to encompass you. With a heart full of gratitude and love, it is time to get to work.

Standing next to the table, in line with your clients heart, reach up toward the sky with open hands and draw down the first beam of energy. This is the heart link, or in Native American tradition, Sowelu. Pull this beam down to your own heart, then raise it up and slightly away from your body in thanks, then bring it down to the area above your client's heart and focus on this linking energy for a minute (Hold your hands in the firm way you learned in week one). You will know your connection has been established when Spirit begins to guide your session.

As you work it is vitally important to be a clear channel. You are simply an energy pathway, or antenna, for healing to occur. An antenna has no opinions or judgements, no religion or prejudices and no belief system whatsoever. As a clear channel, an antenna receives information from every direction and every source of information in the vicinity. As a clear channel you will receive information from many sources. You will simply record what you experience without any interpretation. Enter into each healing session like a wide eyed child, with no expectations or agendas, but rather with excitement about the new adventure that is in front of you.

Once you have thoroughly grounded your client's energy, begin to scan the body for any disturbances or blockages. Thuroughly examine each disturbance in the energy; how does it feel, what does it look like, etc. Also take note of its vibrational frequency. Does it feel slow or heavy or dark? When you feel that you have examined every nuance of the blockage, begin to clear it by bringing love to the fear.

When you feel complete, that you have been guided to all pertinent areas by the guides, begin to clear the chakras. This is done in very much the same way you clear your own chakras. Using the same technique you feel comfortable with when doing your chakra meditation is the best method for clearing another's energy centers as well. Begin with the feet and work your way up to the 12th chakra, taking notes all the way about what you find, how you found it (spirit told you, angel showed you, etc.).

Take notes throughout the session in order to free your mind to focus completely on the next energy disturbance you encounter. As you work, you will find that a great deal of information comes through, and you cannot possibly remember it all. I make frequent trips back and forth from my client to my clip board, so I keep it close.

Be mindful of your posture. Do not sacrifice your health for the health of your client. As you work, keep your natural girdle (abdominal muscles) strong and if you need to bend over, choose to squat instead to preserve your spine.

Protect and seal in your work

Once the chakras are cleared, it is time to surround the client with protective white light from the Universe. Begin by bringing your hands to the top of the 12th chakra and, opening your arms as you pass over the clients body, pull the energy down past the feet and bring your hands together again to cinch it. Fill it with love and know that you are complete.

Move to the client's side and stretch your arms wide to feel the integrity of the egg/bubble of white light you just applied. Examine it visually as well and take note of the difference between how the aura looks now as opposed to how it appeared before the session began.

Bow to the clients BHS, to the Universe and to all who helped you with this session and give them your sincerest thanks and gratitude.

Touch your clients shoulder and welcome them back into the room gently.

In Review:

1. **Clear the space**
2. **Connect to guides**
3. **Ground clients energy**
4. **Seek and clear all blockages**
5. **Examine and clear all chakras**
6. **Surround client in white light from 12 to 0**
7. **Give thanks**

Debriefing your client

Give your client a moment to adjust back to reality and ask them how they feel. Would they like some water? Maybe a tissue? At this point everything is fresh in their mind and you want them to share everything they experienced. Write it all down. Ask open ended questions: What did you feel, see, hear, smell? Did you feel me touch you at any time? Sometimes a spirit will touch the client and it will coincide with some information that you gleaned during the session.

When they are complete, you can begin to tell them about what you found. Be sensitive! If you saw something awful, tell them you saw *something* that had to do with whatever body part it was, and let the client elaborate. If there is an illness in the liver, for example, your client probably already knows about it and this is why they came to you. Tell them that the energy has been cleared and let that be the end of it. This is egoless healing. Remember- you created the path for the healing, but the Spirit and the client did all the actual healing. Do not allow the client to draw illness back to the body by talking about it as if it's still there. Remind them that it has been cleared and encourage them to remember that fact every time they think about it.

If you see a tragic accident, like a head on collision with a big white truck, don't tell your client what you saw. Instead, tell them to remain alert on the road and you might tell them specifically to make sure they stay in their own lane while driving, and certainly not to be a distracted driver. Also, you will never be shown anything you cannot change. This is a *shamanic truth.* There would be no reason for the Universe to show us something if we're powerless to do anything about it. So when you see something like this during a session, move the energy to change the trajectory of the vehicles, for example, and trust that it is done.

If, after sharing all the information you received, your patient asks why you didn't see something about them that they think is obvious, remind them that they have lived for many years, and many lifetimes, and that you only worked with their energy for 30 minutes. Spirit brought forward only the most pertinent information; whatever needed to be addressed on this day.

Closing instructions for the patient

Tell your client that the more rest you have, the more benefit you will gain from the energy. Maintain the high vibration you now have, by appreciating everyone and everything. Continue to mindfully breathe deeply and surround yourself with Universal Love. When you cultivate and remain in this energy, your immune system cannot revert back to illness, and stress can no longer affect your health.

Drink plenty of water to help your body detox and process the work we did today.

The subtle effects of this healing energy are different for everyone. People usually begin to experience changes on the mental and physical levels within a few hours of the session. You may feel lighter and have more energy, or you may feel very tired and need to go home and sleep. Listen to your body. Tell your client that being healed *should* change the mind and body!

As the healing facilitator, the only 'residue' you will be left with is comparable to the sensation of having just made love. The endorphins will be high and you may feel elated! If you remember how the illness of your client felt, know that it is just that; a memory of a sensation. You have not taken it on yourself.

After the session

Turn the heat back on! (I say this because I have forgotten to do this in the past and hours later wondered why I was so cold) and turn your phone/ringer back on. Retrieve the 'Do Not Disturb' sign from your door.

File your Client Request & Authorization sheet with the Debriefing sheet. Do not leave these personal documents laying around. Also, I have found it helpful to scan them and put them into a digital file on my computer where they can be accessed quickly and easily.

In a few days, or weeks, you will most likely get a phone call from your patient telling you that they are better, or that their doctor said "It's gone". It is an incredible blessing to be a part of someone's healing. If that doesn't humble you, nothing ever will.

Distant Healing

There will be times when someone cannot get to you, or you can't get to them, so you will facilitate the SHE session distantly. The process is exactly the same. You make an appointment, decide on the duration of your session, and instruct your client to be lying down and relaxing while you are working on them for the entire time.

Turn on Ardas, prepare yourself as described above, then get seated comfortably. Make the connection to your clients BHS, create your heartlink, then with your eyes closed, follow the guidance you receive to clear the body.

Remember that you are merely a vehicle for the Universe to work through. This work flows from the Divine and can be done anywhere. There are no limitations on healing.

A word about Universal law:

Disease follows laws. If you take poison, you die, no matter who you are. There are always going to be laws of cause and effect. There will always be a consequence for every action, thought, and prayer we put out into the world, and no prayer will break the laws of nature. Your power lies in the decision whether or not to take the poison; your awareness of the poison, but once it's done, it's done.

Sometimes we have written disease into our contract for our growth, and it won't be cleared until that growth has occurred. Remember that the root of all disease, and all health, is in us. It does not come onto the body from outside of us. We can guide the client to the healing path, but ultimately the work is his or hers to do.

Charging for your services

You provide the purest form of healing on the planet. It works on every level, every time, and you deserve to be compensated well for facilitating it.

A one hour session (half hour energy - half hour debriefing): $150.00. This is my preference, as it is very difficult to get everything you need in less than half an hour.

A half hour session (15-20 minutes energy – 10-15 minutes debriefing): $80.00. I will offer this option when a prospective client, who truly needs my help, absolutely cannot do an hour long session, either because of time issues or financial reasons.

Doing this work free of charge is out of integrity. There must be an equal exchange of energy for any healing to take place, and money is energy. Of course you may also barter services.

Types of Clients:

1- Mystery Client: This is the client who comes to you one time, receives their healing, either physical or emotional, and you never hear from them again.

2- Sincere Client: This is the client who feels the need to see you 4-6 times to be sure they have gotten to the bottom of their issues, and this is what I always suggest. This way we can do a thorough job of gleaning information from Spirit, and discussing emotional issues in a further effort to clear them.

3- Regular Client: This is the client who will want to have their energy cleared for them every week, or every other week, as a kind of maintenance program. This client may be trying to clear karma in order to ascend to enlightenment, and because the results of this work are cumulative, each successive visit builds upon the last. I've seen great results in the spiritual ascension of these clients.

Shamanic Healing Energy™ for children

Tell mom or dad that their child can bring a favorite stuffed toy or blanket. Just a little something to make them comfortable on the table.

Have a blindfold/ sleep mask nearby if needed.

Start by chatting to make the child comfortable:

1. "Do you say your prayers at bedtime?" (or any other time). When the child says yes, ask who they pray to, then explain that the angels and other guides who listen to prayers, will be helping us to make him/her healthier and happier.
2. "You can say your prayers while you're on the table, too. Ask for all the angels to come make you feel better, and let them know that you love them very much and thank them for helping you."

With small children, expect the session to be short, as their attention span is limited. Follow your instincts and either end the session when the child wiggles around or gently guide them back into a calm state with soothing words of encouragement.

Practice often on people, plants and even animals, to hone your natural abilities. Before you know it, facilitating Shamanic Healing Energy™ will come naturally to you.

*****

Following are the forms mentioned above. Photo copy the images and have them laminated. Keep them on your clip board with the Client

Request & Authorization and Debriefing forms.

I use these illustrations from Barbara Brennan's Hands of Light to explain the process of a SHE session:

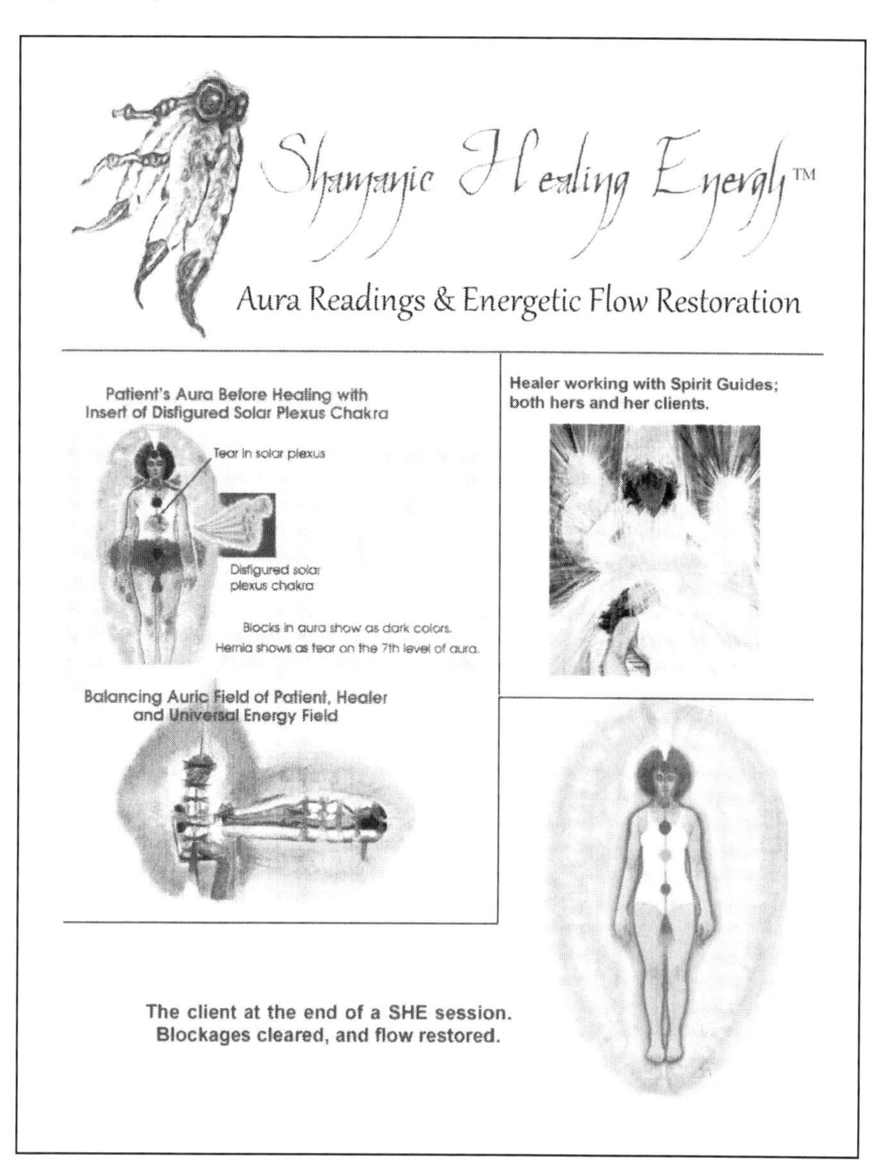

Other useful items to keep on your clip board are reflexology maps, acupuncture maps and even anatomy charts. Things to refer to when Spirit draws you to a specific area of the patient's body.

This sign is for the door to your office:

Please

DO NOT DISTURB!!!

Shamanic Healing Energy

Session in progress

To experience your own Divine Connection
Text or call:

You will have to re-type the following form to personalize it with your name and qualifications.

CLIENT REQUEST AND AUTHORIZATION

I, the undersigned, request that Bonnie M. Russell explain and demonstrate the use of herbs, vitamins, nutrition and energy therapy for the purpose of enhancing my health and for educational purposes. I acknowledge that it is my decision to use or refuse said advice and products.

I understand that Bonnie M. Russell is a certified Master Herbalist, a title which encompasses the fields of herbs, vitamins and nutrition. She is also Nationally Board Certified by the American Association of Drugless Practitioners. She has further earned her Doctor of Shamanism and Master of Spiritual Leadership degrees through the Universal Life Seminary and is certified to provide Integrative Energy Therapy and The Reconnection™.

Bonnie M. Russell, and Shamanic Healing Energy™, make no claims, promises or guarantees, and are neither diagnosing nor treating specific health issues or challenges.

Print Name: ______________________ Today's Date: ____________

Signature: ______________________ Date of Birth: ____________

Phone: ________________ E mail: ______________________

Address: ____

Now is your opportunity
to experience these frequencies.

Shamanic Healing Energy™ Instructions -- Read Carefully

Come in, lie down, close your eyes. Let yourself drift, without falling asleep. Trust that whoever it is that hears your thoughts and prayers has already heard yours. Not only have they already heard what you've asked for, they've also heard what you *haven't thought* to ask for. They've known all along. Even before you walked in. So stop talking, stop the mind chatter, and just listen; let the universe bring you whatever *it* decides you need. Just lie there and be as open to experiencing nothing as you are to experiencing something. In that openness, your experience will arrive.

Client Debriefing form:

The following goes on the top of a standard 8.5 x 11 sheet of paper. Write all of your session notes underneath. In time you will develop a sort of short hand so you can take fast, detailed notes.

Session notes/ Debriefing

Name: ________________ Session # 1 2 3 4 5 Date: __________

Start time: _______ End time: ________ Location ______________

Ended by ___________

What was your experience? What do you recall? (I felt this, I saw that, I heard this, I smelled that) What else do you recall about that? No Impressions--- stick to the facts.
Did I touch you during the session? How did I touch you? (have client demonstrate)

How to be of service with your training in energy medicine

Congratulations on successfully completing the Empowered Empath/Become your own Shaman course! Now that you're a certified to administer Shamanic Healing Energy, how can you really be of service in a practical way?

You can use your new intuitive skill set while working in your current health care profession, such as nursing or massage therapy, to enhance the healing of your clients/clients.

Where you may have only been able to draw blood or administer an IV, you now have the ability to calm and soothe the energy of the client who is experiencing discomfort, on many levels.

The most important use of your skills is going to be in emergency situations.

When someone is involved in an accident, many times the shock of sustaining an injury is worse that the injury itself. Grounding and encouraging the victim becomes vital to the healing process.

A real life example I experienced was a motorcycle accident involving a friend of mine. Approaching the scene, I saw an ambulance and behind it, my friend was strapped to a board on the asphalt. In a flash I saw the events that led to her loss of control, and I saw how she handled herself. I quickly made my way to her side. The moment she saw me, she called my name and smiled, which came as quite a relief! I saw her energy in disarray all around her head, but I noticed that the rest of her body had sustained only superficial wounds.

She was OK.

I knelt down and she took my hand as I directed grounding energy to her spirit. I also told her that she had fallen like a pro and that she should teach others how to fall so gracefully. She smiled broadly and I felt her energy settle back into her body.

The EMT's whisked her away to tend to her physical injuries and it was then that her riding partners shared the events of the accident with me. It was exactly as I had seen it play out in my mind.

Remember that as you grow in your abilities, you will have a much better idea of what your strengths are. Maybe you are perfectly suited for one on one everyday care giving, or perhaps you are more comfortable dealing with strangers. You may find that you can see the energies very clearly and restore balance and flow easily, or you may find that your gifts lie in more in sensing emotional issues. Whatever your specific gifts are, there is a need and I'm confident that you will find your niche.

Occupations in Holistic Health

Since holistic health covers the entire spectrum of mind, body and spirit, the occupational choices are many:

- Minister: officiate weddings, funerals and baptisms
- Therapist: Life coaching, couples counseling or specialize in addiction recovery
- Nutritionist: work in a hospital or nursing home
- Herbalist: treat clients one-on-one, or manufacture herbal remedies
- Personal trainer: Work in a gym or go into business for yourself
- Teach: Share your knowledge with energetic and passionate students in any setting
- Lead seminars: Speak in front of groups about holistic health and motivate others

- Media: Write a book, host a radio or TV show and share your knowledge
- Go into private practice which will allow you to do a little bit of everything you are called to do

Your imagination is really churning now, isn't it? The possibilities seem endless, and the field continues to grow. More and more people are beginning to take charge of their own health, and they are looking for the guidance of a qualified professional to keep them on track.

I have revealed to you many ways in which to connect to your inner wisdom," whispers Medicine Woman, "but if you do not have the love for humanity in your heart, these tools are useless. Trust your body, trust your process, trust your old terrified flesh as she transforms into the body of the rose. The new rose body will enable you to listen to the symphony of the universe through the vibrations of her flesh."

from *Leaving My Father's House*, Marion Woodward

Homework

1. Daily Meditation

2. Nightly Review

3. Review and revise your thesis

4. Three client studies – See three clients and record the sessions. Turn in a copy of your session notes to be assessed for your certification. Note: To protect the privacy of your clients, use their initials on the copies you turn in.

Preparing for your Spirit Quest next week

- Do not ingest anything other than water the day of the ceremony to make sure you are hydrated.
- Purify yourself (bathe)
- Bring a blanket to sit on, your notebook and pen and a bottle of water.
- Something that is precious to you, such as a crystal, bell, wand or keepsake that brings you peace and power. It will be cleansed and recharged during the ceremony.

Suggested Reading:

The Reconnection, Eric Pearl

The Healing Energy Experiments, Gary E. Schwartz, PhD

Quantum Healing, Deepak Chopra

Interview with an Angel, Steven J. Thayer

The Importance of Ceremony in our Modern World

Week Eight

From baptisms to funerals, and everything in between, human beings have always filled their lives with ceremony.

We're going to explore why that is and what makes it so important.

We know that we create our reality with our thoughts. Ceremony helps us to cement those thoughts with specific actions.

Let's use the wedding ceremony as an example. Any two people can say that they love each other and desire to spend the rest of their lives together, but until they go through the ceremony, it is not perceived as real by the community, and it does not feel real to the couple.

You could say that a ceremony, in this instance, is 'putting your money where your mouth is'. Until they do it, and we see it, they are not taken seriously, even in today's world.

Even though we no longer live in a tribal community, we still need to experience the support of our village during the most auspicious occasions in our lives.

Here is a list of some of the most frequently practiced ceremonies that continue in our modern society:

Baptism

Communion

Confirmation

Graduation

Wedding

Funeral

When we look at this list, a few things are made clear; the first is that birth through the age of thirteen are very important years, full of milestones, while graduation and a wedding doesn't follow far behind. Then we notice that there is a significant gap between the time a person marries and the time of their funeral, which isn't really for the deceased so much as it is for their loved ones.

In that gap we face many hardships and crises of faith; therefore the importance of ceremony increases not diminishes. Tribal society has no place for weakness, so they used the power of ceremony regularly to bolster their courage and to reconnect themselves to each other and to their Universal Source.

Without it, modern man experiences depression, physical illness and has a tendency toward violence.

In modern culture, it is important to add ceremonies to celebrate the changing seasons, the fazes of the moon, and ceremonies to help us get through hardships, such as war or the aftermath of any traumatic experience.

We think that we are sophisticated and that we have evolved far from the time of tribal societies, but we're not there yet. It takes many thousands of years for the human being to evolve and adapt to a new environment. The fact is we are only a short century or two removed from those days. This explains why we suffer from loneliness and depression as well as physical illnesses that were unheard of a few generations ago.

We lived and worked very closely with each other. We were never alone and never worried about how we were going to eat or pay rent, because the village took care of the hunting and the housing as a unit. Warriors in the village protected everyone from outside threats and life was good. Everyone had enough, and nobody had more than anyone else. Babies were held up to 80% more than they are today, and they never slept alone. Children played in close groups near the adults and this helped them to adapt into happy, healthy, well-adjusted adults. This harmony kept us happy and healthy throughout our lifetimes.

Modern man lives alone, or in small family units, sometimes going long stretches without seeing extended family and barely acknowledging their neighbors. Each person cares for their own needs, is only responsible for their own selves, and worries all the time about being better and having more than the next guy. We obsess over our personal safety and the safety of all our things.

This way of life is unnatural and causes the body and the mind much distress.

There are three things we can do to fix the situation. One, we can go back to the old ways of living together and providing for each other like one big happy family, (which won't happen overnight, but I believe we will begin to return to something close to it), two, we can seek the wisdom of those who practice intuitive energy therapies, and three, we can participate in ceremony regularly.

Until we return to communal living, we can turn to modern energy workers as they are today's answer to the village shaman. With their highly specialized abilities, a facilitator of light energy brings the body and mind back into balance, draws stress away from the body and creates the environment for healing to occur, many times spontaneously.

When your energetic flow is restored and your aura is cleared, the sensation is akin to that of being totally free and safe. The sensation of being one with everything; being a part of, not just a tribe, but of everything there is.

Take advantage of these highly trained, very wise people in your area because their knowledge and skill can make a profound difference in your life.

The third tool, ceremony, can be as simple as holding a monthly bonfire to celebrate the moon, the season, the harvest, or anything else that strikes your fancy. The emphasis should be on releasing old energy, or habits, that no longer serve us, and to bring in beneficial energies to carry you to the next bonfire ceremony. No special skills are required for these types of ceremony, just a sincerity of the heart.

Modern Shamanic Healers, who are highly trained and experienced facilitators, hold specialized ceremonies, as well. Some involve hallucinogenic herbs which can be dangerous and wreak havoc on your physical body as well as the psyche. Others involve a combination of energy healing and ceremonial purging without the use of psychotropic medicine.

Whichever you choose is your personal decision, however it is my opinion that we have everything we need within us and do not require anything from outside of our own body and mind to have a magical, transformational experience. Any hallucinogenic substance used for any purpose, is a crutch and will only inhibit true inner growth of the spirit.

Social Ceremonies

There are many types of ceremonies that are social and meant to be experienced by the community, such as baptism, confirmation, weddings and funerals. These things all say to the world at large that we 'intend' something. Our integrity is on display to all when we stand up publicly and announce our intentions.

In the case of a baptism, it is the family's intention to raise their child a particular way, or simply to introduce the child to the community before God. Confirmation is a rite of passage that brings a child officially into adulthood by learning the ways of the community or by the accomplishment of some feat. The 13 year old is stating their purpose for all to hear, so that they may assist in holding him or her to their promise. A wedding is a way of saying that you are serious about your commitment to your love. It is putting your money where your mouth is by saying publicly what you feel personally. A funeral is a ceremony that allows loved ones to share their grief and joys over the deceased by telling stories and sharing photos, and by celebrating the life of the departed.

Thinking a thing and doing it in front of witnesses are two very different things. Ceremony is how we express our character and integrity to follow through on a thing.

Objects of Power

The objects that represent holiness to us are important in ceremony. The things that we previously dismissed as impediments to our healing abilities are a vital part of ceremony. This is when we want to wear our jewelry and the clothing that makes us feel like the purest expression of our inner selves.

The baptized baby wears their little gown, the graduate wears a robe with mortar board and tassel and the bride wears white. Without these things the ceremony wouldn't feel complete.

Likewise, when we enter into healing, space clearing and soul retrieval ceremonies we bring our wands and crystals and anything else that brings us power.

Tools of the Trade

First of all let me just say that you are enough. You don't need a single thing outside of yourself to heal others or to be whole yourself.

However, the items that traditionally define the shaman or medicine man or woman have their time and place.

Here are some that I love, and occasionally use myself, all of which come from nature:

- Shaman's Staff – a symbol of strength, usually gifted to the shaman by a teacher, contemporary or from the community that the shaman serves.
- Feathers – Either found or gifted, feathers also have many meanings and uses, not to mention that feathers are an immediately recognized symbol to others that you are on the Red Road.
- Charm bags – All charms that are prepared by and for the shaman are for specific use and have been infused, or charged with the corresponding energy. A love charm, for example, is used only for attracting love and a healing charm is employed only to heal. They are sewn by hand, have hand drawn images on them and contain natural objects that will draw or repel the energy that the bag is intended for.
- Oils and herbs – Used for healing, space clearing and for general maintenance of health and home.

The following items are the type that choose you:

- Crystals – There have been volumes written about the power different crystals and stones, and I encourage you to read a few to get a basic understanding, but the clear quartz crystal is known to be an amplifier of spiritual energy. As such it can be very useful in healing and during ceremony.
- Knives – Specific knives are used in ceremony and in making medicine. Choose one with markings on it that 'speak' to you in some way. Maybe the color or the inlays attract you.
- Findings – stones, bones or other found objects that have a special meaning to you.

All of these tools and sacred objects are to be held in high regard. They are to be kept clean and away from the hands of others. These are personal objects that should only be handled by the practitioner.

Most importantly, have fun with it! When using your tools they should transform your spirit in such a way that you can only bring about healing and peace. When you hold your ceremonial feathers in your hands they should fill you with pleasure and remind you of the day you received them and the spirit in which they were presented to you.

Performing your own Ceremonies

Room Clearing

One of the simplest ceremonies is a room clearing or space clearing.

In a ceramic bowl, place a shovelful of dirt from the northernmost corner of the grounds you wish to clear.

Light your copal packet, smudge, or other holy herbs and place on top of the dirt in your bowl.

Smudge yourself.

Hold the bowl in your recessive hand (if you are right handed, this is your left hand. Your power hand is your right). Using a feather, or a fan, in your power hand, push the smoke away from you into the five directions. Call upon the air of the north, the fire of the east, the earth of the south, the water of the west, then call upon the spirit of the sky.

Set your intention out loud to the five spirits. “I intend to clear all negativity from this space” for example.

Begin to smudge the space in a clockwise fashion, beginning in the northernmost corner of the land. If there is a house or other building, begin in the north corner inside the structure. When the building is complete, return to the north corner of the property and begin to smudge the property line in a clockwise fashion.

As you make your way, continue to push the smoke away from you toward the corners and walls and into closets. Take special care to cleanse all openings, such as windows and doors inside a building, and gates and other entrances when clearing a property.

When you return to the northernmost corner, pour the contents of your bowl into the hole you took the dirt from and cover it over, moving the dirt with your bare hands. Place your hands on the mound and say a thank you or small prayer in acknowledgement that your purpose has been realized, and that the space is indeed, clear.

New Moon Bonfire

A simple ceremony that is perfect for introducing even the most novice to the concepts of gathering together and clearing energy. Great young and old and for men and women of all backgrounds.

The new moon brings powerful energies, and it is a time to put our effort into being happier and lighter, and to reach out to grab the life we have always dreamed of living.

On the new moon we can release old, stagnant ways that keep us stuck in unproductive patterns. Then bring in bright, shiny, new energies from the Universe that will increase our awareness of our connection to each other, and everything else in nature.

Sounds good, but how?

Write down the things that you would like to release: jealousy of a co-worker, anger towards an in-law, quit smoking, or whatever negative habit that occupies your mind, and ruins the quality of your life. On the new moon, hold the intention in your heart-consciousness to let these things go, then burn the list. Fire is a powerful cleansing tool, and you'll be amazed at how real the energy is. Once you KNOW that it is done, that these things are gone from your life, take a deep breath (or three) and begin to bring in the positive energy of Universal Love. As your heart expands with the fullness of this beautiful, new energy, begin to send it to your loved ones. Then send it to those you have had conflict with in the past (but no longer have because you just released it), and so on until you are surrounding the Earth with the brilliant glow of this white light of Universal Love.

Do this every new moon to prepare for the new age of Universal Love which began at the end of 2012. If you're keen, you can feel this energy already, and if you haven't felt it yet, that's even more reason to do this exercise every month.

A great way to raise our consciousness together, and be the change we all want to see in others. On the new moon we begin with our own hearts.

Some Words of Wisdom

"If you want to awaken all of humanity, then awaken all of yourself. If you want to eliminate the suffering in the world, then eliminate all that is dark and negative in yourself. Truly, the greatest gift you have to give is that of your own self-transformation." ~Lao Tzu

"Your vision will become clear only when you can look into your own heart. Who looks outside, dreams; who looks inside, awakes." ~Carl Jung

"By harmonizing with the resonance of Divinity that unites the multidimensional aspects of your identity, you open the gateways of ascension." ~A Journey to Oneness, by Rasha

Healing Ceremonies

What you come into this life to work on, the things you have written into your blueprint for this incarnation, you play out with parents, then, with friends, lovers, business partners, teachers, and with issues in health, wealth, and creative expression. If you begin working with ascended masters or guides, you will work these things out with them because these issues are the basic issues you have with Source. After sufficient processing at the parent/ inner-child and relationship (etc.) level, this core drama with Source surfaces and can be dealt with head on. Source will unconditionally allow us to go round and round, lifetime after lifetime, until the issue is resolved. Until we finally understand that pure love was always available to us and we can finally acknowledge it as yours.

Major life changes happen when an issue that surfaces is clearly about your relationship with Source. When you sense your connection to the Creator and recognize her within yourself, something clicks. Life suddenly makes sense and all of our drama and disease can be released.

Ceremony is an important tool in moving through the process of both recognizing and clearing the issues.

Ceremony suspends repression and allows us a space of utter and complete concentration and reflection. In this space the Creator consciousness will bring forward the themes of your life. They will come to you as nagging thoughts that we typically think of a 'distractions'. Instead of becoming flustered and annoyed by these thoughts, focus on them as they come. Embrace your distraction and surround it with love, no matter what it is. By doing this you come into harmony with the energy of the thing to increase your understanding of whatever it is.

Remember to be a non-attached observer, without emotion. Pass no judgement on yourself or on your thoughts. Once you have absorbed it; made it a part of yourself, its power becomes diffused. When a thing no longer has power over you, you are free of it!!!

> For example, if you have cancer in your body, one of the hardest things for a person to come to terms with is the fact that the cancer serves as a messenger. Embrace the cancer. Examine it. Look at its roots. Ask it questions until you are satisfied that you know it completely. If you become overwhelmed and back away, it will wait for you to come back around to it in the future. It won't go away until you do. This is why the scientific community will only say that a cancer is in remission, and not cured. It can be cut from the body, but it will return if it is not consciously dealt with. If you deal with it thoroughly right now, it will be completely diffused and assimilated.

Other issues will come, and as they do, continue to examine them all the way through until you are intimately acquainted with every nuance. Then surround it with love and absorb it.

Ceremony brings us to God Consciousness, as layer upon layer of our fears and inhibitions are released. Something important to know as we do this work is that our BHS, our higher consciousness, will not push us further than we can go. Nothing will surface that we are unable to deal with. *If you can feel it, you can heal it!*

Your honesty with each issue as it surfaces will facilitate faster and smoother assimilation and healing. Integrity is at the heart of this process (surprise!), as it is in everything else we ever do in this life.

The Spirit Quest Ceremony

The purpose of the Spirit Quest ceremony is soul retrieval. We go to deal with the issues that keep us in this manufactured world and separate us from the real (spirit) world. Our only sin, the only thing that keeps us from God consciousness, is the illusion that our flesh is real, and therefore, that the struggles of the flesh are real. We spirit quest to release ego by humbling ourselves before the Universal Source of all things. We do this as a group to support and acknowledge the progress of the other parts of ourselves and to reinforce the fact that 'All are One.'

Preparing for your Spirit Quest

- Do not ingest anything other than water the day of the ceremony to make sure you are hydrated.
- Purify yourself (bathe)
- Bring: a blanket to sit on, a notebook and pen and a bottle of water.
- Something that is precious to you, such as a crystal, bell, wand or keepsake that brings you peace and power. It will be cleansed and recharged during the ceremony.
- Use the restroom before entering the circle.
- Smudge yourself upon entering the circle with copal, sage, or any combination of high holy herbs, and ground your energy through your feet and hands until you feel an inner calmness in your heart. All chatter ceases.
- Moving clockwise around the circle (or fire) three times, draw energy up through the earth and down from the sky. Feel these energies entwine within every cell in your body.
- Welcome the Divine, call the four corners (or anything that your chosen path deems necessary).
- Administer Maya Cacao, an ancient spiced dark chocolate drink that is used to focus concentration.
- Sit quietly and reverentially, prepared to address an issue. Once you are in the circle, you are in sacred space. Even though we are all together, each one of us will be going on a

highly personal, individual journey and no interruption of another's energy will be permitted.

- As we go into silence, allow your expectation and excitement to grow. You will return from this journey with a new perspective.
- Upon resolution, rise and silently give thanks to the Universal Source of all things.
- Come out of the circle, ground any residual energy, then affirm that you have been heard by saying, "So shall it be."
- Write your experience down in your notebook while it is fresh.

When everyone is complete, we'll share our insights with the group and receive tokens to commemorate the experience.

Graduation Ceremony

Presentation of certificates and celebration

Suggested Reading:

Below are a few books that will bring you greater clarity about your divine nature

Bringers of the Dawn: Teachings from the Pleiadians by Barbara Marciniak
Interview with an Angel, Steven J. Thayer
Co-creating at It's Best, A Conversation Between Master Teachers, Wayne Dyer and Esther Hicks

Dearest Student,

Thank you for coming on this journey with me. It has been my honor and my pleasure to share this time and this information with you. I hope you will follow up by reading the suggested titles at the close of each chapter, to gain deeper insight into the subjects we only touched upon.

It is my most fervent desire that you will come to a place in your spiritual journey where you are so completely full; so satisfied by all that you have learned, that you simply must stop learning and start teaching. That is what happened to me and I cannot express how much that shift has changed my life. This does not mean I have stopped learning! Far from it! But I have shifted from being a vessel to being a circuit. I find that I am no longer satisfied to only fill myself. Instead, I share every new morsel of spiritual guidance with all who share an interest.

It is only through the egoless sharing of all knowledge, that the world will be transformed.

Much Love,

Bonnie

Bonnie M. Russell

ABOUT THE AUTHOR

About Rev. Dr. Bonnie M. Russell

Bonnie is a minister and Holistic Health Practitioner, nationally board certified by the American Association of Drugless Practitioners, a Doctor of Shamanistic Theology and a Master Herbalist. These degrees fully encompass the fields of herbs, vitamins, and nutrition, as well as spiritual and emotional health. Additionally, she is an ACE certified Personal Trainer and a SCW certified Yoga Instructor.

It is her goal to bridge the gap between physical health and spiritual connection for her clients. As a speaker and teacher and in private practice since 1998, she explains the link between these subjects in her book, "Spirit Flight, Claim Your Joy and Your Health Will Follow" and in her course, "The Empowered Empath, Become your own Shaman".

AllOne is a ministry of health and healing, devoted to a holistic approach to all things, in every community.

Blossom Spring Natural Health Solutions®

Bonnie's company, *Blossom Spring*, is a line of herbal remedies that are the result of generations of research and development. Our formulas are synergistic combinations designed to complement each other for the maximum performance of each plant. Based on centuries of herbal wisdom, our products are the perfect marriage of modern, scientific knowledge and traditional herbal practices.

Just the way it was when time began.

Just as nature intended it to be.

Notes

Notes

Printed in Poland
by Amazon Fulfillment
Poland Sp. z o.o., Wrocław

31864235R00098